MEMOIRS OF A LEAVISITE:

The decline and fall of Cambridge English

Memoirs
of a Leavisite

The decline and fall of
Cambridge English

David Ellis

LIVERPOOL UNIVERSITY PRESS

First published 2013 by
Liverpool University Press
4 Cambridge Street
Liverpool
L69 7ZU

British Library Cataloguing-in-Publication data
A British Library CIP record is available

ISBN 978-1-84631-889-4 cased

Typeset in Chaparral by Carnegie Book Production, Lancaster
Printed and bound by CPI Group (UK) Ltd, Croydon CR0 4YY

For Geneviève

We talk so grandly, in capital letters, about *Mornings in Mexico*. All it amounts to is one little individual looking at a bit of sky and trees, then looking down at the page of his exercise book.

D. H. Lawrence

Cette effroyable quantité de *Je* et de *Moi!* Il y a de quoi donner de l'humeur au lecteur le plus bénévole.

Stendhal

Ridiculous the waste sad time
Stretching before and after

T. S. Eliot

CONTENTS

Preface   xi

1   Holloway   1

2   First Impressions   7

3   Sanctimonious prick?   15

4   Close reading   22

5   Time out   30

6   QDL   37

7   Class   44

8   Politics   51

9   France   59

10 The Richmond lecture   67

11 Loose end   74

12 Research   82

13 Theory   90

14 Australia   98

15 Shakespeare, Stendhal and James Smith   106

16 Teaching in the UK   114

17   Lawrence   121

18   … and Eliot   129

19   Epilogue   137

Acknowledgements   145
Index   147

PREFACE

For most of those now teaching English in schools or universities, Leavis is an irrelevance; for those being taught he could be said – in an expression he himself favoured – not to exist. The writing was already on the wall twenty years ago when the Council for University English sent a deputation to the Minister for Education and then complained that his point of view was that of an 'unreconstructed Leavisian'. This was a clear enough signal that the project Leavis had launched in the 1920s had failed, in part because of social changes he could never have fully anticipated, but also on account of flaws in the project itself. Yet in the years leading up to the Second World War, and for three or four decades afterwards, his influence was crucial in defining what the teaching of English ought to be. A measure of his success was that, to what must have been the extreme irritation of those of his Cambridge colleagues who taught the subject in a different way, the expression 'Cambridge English' was widely understood to mean only one thing. Leavis's approach gave the subject a coherence it has not since possessed or indeed appeared to want, diversity being the quality which, by accident or design, now seems more highly valued.

This book deals with the decline and fall of Cambridge English, its rise being a phenomenon of which I have no personal experience. The topic strikes me as important because English, in the sense of English literature, remains a major national concern. Millions of pounds of public money are spent on teaching it at both secondary and tertiary level, and a large section of the publishing industry would wither away if that teaching stopped. Many of those who review new books for the newspapers and magazines, or comment on them for the radio or television, read English at university, and what they have to say helps determine the quality of our cultural life. Literature may now play a subsidiary role in that life but language is still central to it so that the varieties of linguistic achievement the critics recommend, and the words they use in making their recommendations, remain significant.

There is already an admirably thorough study of *Scrutiny*, the critical journal by means of which Leavis and his collaborators disseminated their views between 1932 and 1953; and more than one book on Leavis himself. This one is different in that it is a memoir of being taught by him in the early 1960s. What I have tried to do is consider the extent to which I was representative, in training and social background, of the kind of pupil Leavis taught in that period and describe the effect his teaching had on me. My personal details are included only in so far as they contribute to that aim. The advantage of this approach is that it makes no pretence to being either objective or comprehensive. If there are aspects of his work and personality I have neglected, it is because I did not notice them, or they did not strike me as important. Apart from the danger that some of those with experience similar to mine might find my response to Leavis idiosyncratic, the *disad*vantage is one associated with all writing of an autobiographical cast. The readers of a memoir are almost inevitably bound to see in it a self different from the one its author meant to present, by-passing the deliberately stated in order to arrive at the inadvertently revealed. There is (that is) no way of writing its lines so close together that someone else can not read between them. To describe my own experience is therefore much more of a self exposure, or self betrayal, than I can ever know. Yet since my general intention is to explain what it means to be or have been a Leavisite, there is no reason why this occluded or second self, which the reader discovers, should not also be enrolled to bear witness.

ONE

HOLLOWAY

I can remember listening to a conversation which took place outside the house of John Newton, one of my Cambridge supervisors. The only other person present was Harold Mason, who had been an editor of *Scrutiny* and a staunch collaborator of Leavis in the 1940s. Sometime in the mid-1950s, Mason had left Cambridge in order to teach English in Exeter but he had recently reappeared as the holder of the F. R. Leavis Lectureship. This was a post that Newton and others had succeeded in establishing after there had been a public appeal for the necessary funds. The idea was that, with his retirement imminent, there should be some way of continuing Leavis's work in Cambridge, the reasonable assumption being that most of those with power and influence in the university would be only too pleased to see the back of him. But the appointment of Mason did not meet with Leavis's approval, and still less with that of his wife, so that the result was a degree of acrimony exceptional even by the high standards Cambridge set in these matters.

I am reasonably sure of the date of this conversation because Newton and Mason were discussing a memoir which John Holloway, one of the members of the Cambridge Faculty, had just published. To say that Holloway was on Leavis's black list would not do much to distinguish him since that was true of most of those who held permanent posts in the English Faculty in the early 1960s. When I was his pupil, there were very few of his colleagues for whom he had a good word. He would occasionally point wryly to himself and say *cet animal est méchant*, optimistically assuming that his hearers would be able to complete the quotation. It took me a while to realise that these words were the beginning of a French witticism which continues *quand on l'attaque, il se défend*, and certainly there were always those willing to cast the first stone. In 1956, about ten years before the incident I am recalling, Holloway had given a couple of talks on the BBC's third programme called 'The New "Establishment" in Criticism' and complained that 'the regime of close reading' had become mechanical and was not in any case applicable to long works. Only a few months before his memoir appeared, he had published in *The Cambridge Review* an article entitled 'The Dead Straight Dodo Bat: English in Cambridge'. This began by suggesting that because graduate studies were expanding so rapidly, the English Faculty could no longer afford to administer them in its usual amateur fashion; but Holloway went on to tell the world that, in recent meetings of the relevant committee, Leavis had spoken out against research proposals involving Joyce and Pound. Since he was the only Cambridge academic mentioned in the article, the obvious implication was that Leavis was the dodo referred to in its title. When he protested about the impropriety of repeating outside a university committee room words heard within it, Holloway accused him of being willing to air opinions in private which he was not prepared to defend in public.

At the beginning of his career, Holloway had taught philosophy in Oxford and become a fellow of All Souls. Ian Jack, who was also hostile to Leavis, had similarly migrated from Oxford to Cambridge; but there were plenty of other enemies without Oxonian connections. The colleague I remember as being his particular *bête noire* was Graham Hough. Beyond the fact that he felt he had been forced into hurrying the publication of *D. H. Lawrence: Novelist* because Hough was about to steal his ideas, I never discovered the precise reasons for this animosity. A fanciful mind might have said that Leavis and Hough ought to have got on well because they were both war victims. But the wars in question were of course different. The widely recognised irritability of Hough was popularly attributed in Cambridge to his being trapped in Singapore when the Japanese invaded and having therefore had to spend the rest of the Second World War in one of their camps. Leavis was just finishing school when World War One broke out and because there were in his family ideological objections to British foreign policy (his father had been defiantly pro-Boer), he joined the Friends' Ambulance Brigade, without being himself a Quaker or indeed a Christian. He arrived in France at the start of the Somme offensive and spent the rest of the war on an ambulance train, ferrying wounded or dying soldiers back from clearing stations near the front line to the French ports. It was a harrowing experience which had occasionally led him (he once told an ex-pupil) to wish that some of his more severely wounded charges could be spared further suffering and die, and which left him, when he returned to England, with a ruined digestion, insomnia and a stutter, extremely reluctant to talk about his time in France for fear of dishonouring the memory of those who had not come back. In an essay he wrote late in his life, he described meeting an ingenuous young American who, when the wholesale slaughter during the war of young British officers was being discussed, glibly referred to 'the death wish'. Leavis explains how he just did not know what to say:

> What actually came out was, 'They didn't want to die'. I felt I couldn't stop there, but how to go on. 'They were brave' – that came to me as a faint prompting, but no; it didn't begin to express my positive intention; it didn't even lead towards it. I gave up; there was nothing else to do.

These words convey effectively a painful dilemma even if 'death wish', grotesquely inappropriate though it may be in the context Leavis describes, is not too inaccurate a phrase to describe the feelings which develop in the protagonist of that long short story by Lawrence he very much admired, 'England my England'.

It is always hard to know what influence ought to be attributed to traumatic experiences, whether, for example, Leavis's war experiences helped to make him a tough and combative individual, or it was because he was already tough and combative that he was able to survive them. Certainly, when it came to controversy, and attacks as apparently unprovoked and gratuitous as Holloway's, he was both formidable and fearless, well able to look after himself. As his pupil, I inherited many of his dislikes without the means to sustain them. By the time the conversation about Holloway I am remembering took place, I must already have been a research student. I did not submit the Ph.D. I was working on until I came back from Australia in 1971 and was then startled to be told that Hough would be one of my examiners. The image that came into my mind was from *Here to Eternity*, a film which had been popular in the 1950s. This was not the most obvious one of Burt Lancaster and Deborah Kerr clasped passionately together and rolling in the surf on some beach in Hawaii. I certainly remembered that, as almost every adolescent male of my generation also did, partly perhaps because Kerr, in her one-piece bathing suit, had previously been best known for playing demure ladies from the English upper classes. But on this occasion the moment from the film which had impressed me and now came rushing back was when Frank Sinatra, who plays a cocky, authority-defying army private, is led into the stockade and greeted by the gloating sergeant in charge, Ernest Borgnine. Sinatra has previously had a tussle with Borgnine, who usually managed to look spectacularly evil (even if he did once play Marnie), and has been warned that the time for revenge will one day come. It would be foolish of me to offer here my own explanations of why I have always been impressed by these scenarios in films and books in which some heedless action, or even some insult to others of which one may not at the time have been aware, has catastrophic consequences. Beyond being friendly with his au pair, I was not conscious of ever having done anything to offend Hough, but I certainly knew that I had participated in Leavis's hostile feelings towards him. In the event, it may have been largely thanks to Hough that I was awarded the Ph.D. Intellectually unadventurous, my thesis had become over time very limited in scope. This was a weakness (I later learned) which troubled my younger, 'external' examiner but his hesitations were dismissed by Hough who was perhaps keen to show that all the ill-feeling which existed between him and Leavis would not stop him being fair to one of Leavis's pupils. The result strengthened a feeling I have always had that the relation between individual effort and achievement can often be tortuously indirect. 'And so we plough together', says Aesop's flea as he sits in the ear of the ox.

What Mason was saying to Newton about Holloway's memoir concerned the chapter in which he describes being brought up in a household that was virtually bookless, and indeed almost without 'culture' of any kind. It strikes me now that his remarks could have had several different meanings. He might have been suggesting that Holloway's childhood was one more illustration of the way in which, according to Leavis, the old 'organic' communities of the former agricultural villages and towns had been broken up by the incursions of capitalism and left behind a working population that was rootless, alienated and culturally deprived. Alternatively, he might merely have been noting how well Holloway had managed to do in spite of the social disadvantages of his childhood (between leaving Oxford and taking up a fellowship in Cambridge, he had been Byron Professor of English in Athens). But the *tone* I remember does not suggest either of these interpretations. That indicates rather that Mason felt Holloway had given himself away and been found out: that in describing how he had been brought up, he had revealed to the world why he was such an unsatisfactory individual. I assume that I have remembered his remarks in this way because I also came from a bookless home and always obscurely felt that someone would soon discover that Cambridge was a place where I had no right to be, and to which I did not belong.

Whether the moments we happen to remember do in fact have a particular meaning and are not random and arbitrary products of the nervous system, must (I imagine) be a moot point; but anyone who tries to write a memoir has to believe in their significance. I associate what Mason said about Holloway, or the tone in which I remembered him saying it, with a remark I read a year or two later in Sainte-Beuve. This was when I was in Paris, pursuing my research, and following Matthew Arnold's recommendation about the superiority of French literary criticism. I have in general very little feeling for books as material objects – any old paperback will do – but in this case I had seen and bought a nineteenth-century edition of Sainte-Beuve's complete works, fifty or so volumes of mostly his weekly articles (only when I began ploughing through them did I realise why they were so cheap). I never succeeded in reading them all but paid special attention to what Sainte-Beuve had to say about Balzac, a writer he once described as his *proie preferée*. For many years Balzac scrabbled about in the lower reaches of literature, only finally establishing himself with *La Peau de chagrin*, that story about a young man who buys a magic piece of shagreen which gives him vital powers but ominously contracts each time he chooses to use them. It may not have been about this novel but some other that Sainte-Beuve cuttingly observed that anyone who had spent as long as Balzac finding a style could never be sure he was going to keep it. I suppose what Mason said about Holloway outside John Newton's house suggested that certain initial disadvantages could never be overcome while Sainte-Beuve reminded me that any victory over them was only ever likely to be temporary.

Holloway's memoir is called *A London Childhood* and it was only very many years later that I bothered to read it. It struck me then that he ought to have been sympathetic to me since, apart from the bookless home, there were a number of similarities between his background and mine. His mother was a headmaster's daughter whereas the father of mine worked in a cotton waste factory before the First World War but was able to take it over when its German owners either fled the country or were interned. This factory eventually burned down so that, because it was inadequately insured (a detail associated in family lore with my grandfather's Scottish ancestry), he was only moderately well-off when I knew him, but my mother must nevertheless have been brought up in relative comfort, as must Holloway's. Both women then married men who were below them in the social scale and had less education. The difference is that while my father worked in an office all his life, eventually becoming the person who collected orders for the dyeing and proofing of material from local firms and tried to ensure they were promptly fulfilled, Holloway's was an authentic member of the Proletariat who stoked the boiler in a London hospital. In his memoir, he is nevertheless keen to point out that his small terraced home was 'well below the bottom of the middle class', which it no doubt was in spite of two of its rooms being rented out to strangers. And yet there were in his background (as in mine) virtually no visits to concerts or museums, as well as no books; and no influential contacts to smooth his path in life. When I read some of the fascinating memoirs from the 1980s, T. C. Worsley's *Flannelled Fool*, for example, or John Gale's *Clean Young Englishman*, I am struck by the way their authors refer to themselves as 'middle class' even though they were sent by their parents to expensive public schools, and had in their families judges or stockbrokers. It makes me feel that there are gradations in the term which are hardly provided for by the addition of the word 'lower'.

In reading Holloway's book I ought, as I say, to have found him sympathetic and felt more than guilty than I already did about having taken over so easily Leavis's dislike of him. Yet the truth is that I thought the personality which emerged from his memoir somewhat cold and repellent and that it confirmed rather than contradicted the impression I had taken from occasionally hearing him lecture. Here is one of two major features of memoir writing. The first is very simply put by Stendhal when he says, 'Car tout ce que je vous raconte, je l'ai vu; et si j'ai pu me tromper en le voyant, bien certainement, je ne vous trompe point en vous le disant', a remark which could be very roughly paraphrased as meaning that, although he cannot vouch for the truth of what he has recorded, he has tried to put down as accurately as he can what he happens to remember. The second feature is that, as I suggested in my preface, the 'self' the author attempts to present is never the one the reader perceives (cold and repellent not being the impression that I imagine Holloway intended to make). I was once very interested in this topic and marvelled at the way in which, in his *Confessions*, Rousseau is able to anticipate his readers' responses and reveal the most discreditable aspects of himself while still retaining their interest and sympathy. But even he is not exempt from the iron rule.

TWO

FIRST IMPRESSIONS

I used to think that practically all Leavis's pupils must (like me) have come from grammar schools, but there was in fact quite a strong contingent from those largely non-boarding but fee-paying establishments that lay between the State sector at one extreme and Eton or Harrow at the other (Dulwich College, with its large number of pupils on local or county scolarships, would be one example). I was born in an unlovely suburb called Swinton and Pendlebury, which lies about four miles out of Salford on the road from Manchester towards the coast. My grammar school was in Whitefield, at a similar distance from Manchester, but to the north rather than the west. Close by was the suburb of Prestwich, where many of the region's more prosperous Jews lived so that Stand Grammar School (as we were called) was saved from the cultural uniformity of its rival establishments by a large number of Jewish boys. The novelist Howard Jacobson was one of these but since he is three years younger than I am, and three years during schooldays might just as well be ten, I did not get to know him well until we found ourselves at Downing together. I ought by rights to have left before he arrived, but at the time I was offered my place it was assumed that I would only take it up after I had spent two years in the Army, Navy or Air Force, completing my 'national service'.

National service was abolished just as I was about to undertake it, so that I was then left with a couple of years in which I had to occupy myself as best I could. Whether Leavis spontaneously wrote to me with a list of books I ought to read during this waiting period or I had the courage to approach him for advice, I can't remember. The main contents of the letter he sent me I can't remember either, which suggests they were of a kind which would become familiar to me later and which represented Leavis's powerfully distinctive view of what mattered most in the history of English literature. Two curiosities in his list do however stick in my mind. One was Alexandre Beljame's *Men of Letters and the English Public in the Eighteenth Century*. Beljame died in 1906 so in the late 1950s this work was hardly cutting edge; but I imagine Leavis had found it helpful when in the 1920s he was doing his own Ph.D. work on Addison and Steele. The other curiosity was Lord Raglan's *The Hero*, or perhaps it was *Jocasta's Crime*. Its presence in the letter suggests to me that Jane Harrison's *Ancient Art and Ritual* was also there and that these gestures towards anthropology had been provoked by T. S. Eliot's *The Waste Land*, a key text for Leavis, not least because it reinforced and helped him to articulate his own, deeply pessimistic view of modern culture.

I should have set to and worked my way through all the books Leavis recommended and I still don't fully understand why I didn't. For the first year of my two year break I went back to my own primary school as an unqualified and wholly incompetent teacher. It was called Cromwell Road (after its location) and made me feel, when I arrived in Cambridge and discovered how often Leavis was contrasted with his Cavalier enemies in Oxford and elsewhere, that I must have been a Roundhead from the very beginning. My experiences at Cromwell Road were much like those of Ursula Brangwen's at Brinsley Street Elementary in *The Rainbow*, when she goes straight from school into teaching. This was even to the extent of my headmaster also coming periodically into my class room, telling my pupils that their work was disgracefully untidy, and then stalking out, having successfully destroyed any small vestiges of authority I might once have had. The major difference was that I never had to resort to violence as she does. My class was called 4c and consisted of about forty pupils who were not even being 'put in' for the 'eleven plus', the examination which in those days, and educationally speaking, was meant to separate the sheep from the goats. What I find hard to understand now, is why so many children who might have been justifiably resentful at being regarded as educational rejects, and who had been placed in an inappropriate educational context where they were being taught practically nothing by a callow youth, did not give me more trouble. It is true that my discipline was poor with my class often noisy and sometimes chaotic when I followed the fashion of having them work in groups; but if the situation had been as bad as circumstances indicated it ought to have been, the headmaster would have intervened more often than he did. That I survived without the violent measures Ursula feels she has to resort to, I can only attribute to some mysterious coping mechanism having kicked in, and the good nature, or philosophical resignation, of the majority of my pupils.

When I think that most of the girls and boys I was supposed to be instructing must still be alive, I can nevertheless only feel profoundly sorry about how little good I did them.

During my second free year, I did a number of different jobs. For four months, for example, I worked on the night shift at Kellogg's. My main task on the production line was to watch six metal chutes empty cereal into a relay of six packets beneath and make sure the system did not jam. If it did, the chutes would carry on pouring out cornflakes at thirty second intervals without there being anything there to receive them. Very occasionally I was allowed to sit at the head of the line, open out one flattened cardboard package after another, and slide it on to the oblong metal phalanges which were rhythmically appearing on the conveyer belt at my right. Once the cardboard had been slipped on the oblong metal, it would move forward to be sealed underneath and then have inserted into it the greaseproof inner bag. The operation required more manual dexterity than I possessed and the result was often that, as in Chaplin's *Modern Times*, I found myself unable to keep up with the machine and several phalanges would then go by that had nothing on them. Failure in this operation would sometimes mean that I was relegated to the most menial of all the tasks on the assembly line: placing a plastic toy in each packet as it went by. Toys were not always given away, which was a mercy because there was no machine for distributing them. It was easy to become distracted and overlook a package or two. In addition to the pupils in 4c at Cromwell Road therefore, I also feel bad about the numerous children who must have opened their cereal packets at this time and felt deflated to find that the advertised toy was missing.

My fellow employees at Kellogg's were an interesting group. One man explained to me that he liked the night shift because he did not get on with his wife and this way he only saw her when he was coming home from his work and she was going out to hers. He was a member of the permanent core but there was a large floating population of people like myself. The atmosphere was relaxed and friendly thanks to an excellent canteen and also perhaps a certain satisfaction which comes from working when everyone else is asleep. I liked it for a while but the unnaturalness of the regime eventually wore me down. It struck me afterwards that it would have been perfect for several of my fellow students at Cambridge who did their reading and writing through the night and were never up before mid-day. This was Byron's routine, as it was also that of Simon Gray. In his excellent 'Smoking Diaries', Gray often pictures himself at breakfast with his wife, sharing what for him was a final meal before sleep and, for her, a first one after it. But this arrangement was not the same as that of the man at Kellogg's in that it had nothing to do with marital discord. Quite the contrary.

The people at Kellogg's were of a different type from those I met on two other jobs I did at this time; one was the inevitable *rite de passage* on a building site and the other involved cleaning up ditches round Manchester as an entirely supernumerary member of a small gang employed by Manchester City Council for that purpose. Neither was ideal preparation for going to Cambridge and from the moment of leaving school I lost ground rather than gained it. But at least I grew two years older, and age makes what is perhaps always the most significant contribution to the educational process. Given how wide variations in male development can be, I was still, when I arrived in Downing, several years short of the maturity I needed to take advantage of all that was on offer there. The college owes its name to the man who built Downing Street and consists of an unusually large quadrangle of grass with what seemed to me at the time rather dull, uniform eighteenth-century buildings on three sides (I was told later that they represented 'some of Wilkins's best work'). There had been a plan to complete the enclosure of the quadrangle with a fourth side but that had not happened and the fact that one could look out from it towards yet more grass, and the spire of the nearby Catholic Church, gave the whole college a pleasantly open, airy feel. This was an appropriate setting for its famous English Fellow who was well known for wearing sandals and a shirt open to the level of his sternum. His jacket and flannels were very well worn and he had the 'brown baked' look of Eliot's 'familiar compound ghost' in *Little Gidding*, so that when I first saw Leavis I might well have mistaken him for W. H. Davies, the Super-Tramp, if at the time I had known who W. H. Davies was. One of his former pupils does in fact describe how Leavis had arrived at a seminar one morning and said that he had just been stopped on his way into college by a young policeman who suspected him of 'vagrancy'. But that was a foolish mistake given the spring that was always in his step and a gaze which, far from wandering, appeared perpetually alert and penetrating. His features were certainly weather-beaten but seemed to be refined by constant intellectual effort rather than coarsened by booze. In his youth, and before he lost his hair, Leavis must in fact have been quite handsome, although always slight. His ruined digestion gave him no way of being able to increase his bulk but it helps explain the special, humorous pleasure with which he would recall the claim De Quincey made, sometime in the 1840s, that for reasons which had nothing to do with war service, he had not enjoyed a square meal since the eighteenth century.

American universities are notorious for attracting students with names of famous intellectuals who then prove to be on semi-permanent sabbatical leave. Nothing could be less like the situation at Downing for those stud-ying English. I saw a lot of Leavis because he spent one hour with our year (about ten students), three times a week. He did the same with years two and three so that he had racked up nine of what are now known as 'contact hours' before he began thinking of what else he might have to do. A year or two before I arrived, he had been seeing each year four times a week. Since he always manifested the same degree of vitality in our meetings, I suspect that the change was not his initiative but was made because it was found that the *students* could not keep up the pace; and attendance at his seminars was as it happens patchy. Apart from the one or two who would have done well at Kellogg's and did not get up in time, there were those who found the content of them far too familiar. Almost all my fellow students had been taught by men who were either former pupils of Leavis or very sympathetic to his point of view. At my own school, the English teaching had not made much impression on me until the arrival, just as I was entering the sixth form, of a charismatic new master. He was tall with a mass of black hair Brylcreemed back in the Dennis Compton fashion and would have been good-looking if his nose had not been set slightly askew. When one of Lincoln's political opponents accused him of being two-faced, he apparently asked whether he would look like he did if he had had a choice. In a somewhat similar spirit my English master replied, when I once asked him if he had ever done any boxing, 'Well you don't think I was born with this nose, do you?', although I imagine he was. His mouth turned up at one corner in a sardonic grimace, and sardonic humour was his trademark. What made him particularly appealing to us was that he was a local boy from Oldham (I think I heard his father kept a shop). Part of his appeal was that he gave a strong impression of keeping an ironic distance from the whole business of schoolmastering, and of only passing through.

Derek Beard, as this new English master was called, made me enthusiastic about literature but he was certainly not a Leavisite. At Oxford he had been taught by that same Ian Jack who, on his move to Cambridge, became one of the most virulent of Leavis's antagonists. He must have familiarised us with aspects of Leavisian thinking when we were studying *Paradise Lost*: one could hardly teach that text then without alluding to the controversy Leavis had started by suggesting that being able to write Latin just as easily as he wrote English was no necessary advantage to Milton, and that although in certain passages his rhythms might be appropriate, they had in the main a tendency to become mechanical and boring. But I cannot remember any striking endorsements of Leavis and I had not read any of the key texts – *New Bearings in English Poetry, Revaluation, The Great Tradition, The Common Pursuit* – before I went to Downing. Even today I am not sure whether I have ever properly read these books, rather than heard them recited. I do not mean here that in his seminars Leavis gave them to us word for word, but as I was able to establish later by judicious flicking, he did offer us the gist and with what were, crucially, many of the same examples. Although this must have irritated some of my contemporaries and helps to explain their occasional absences from the seminars, I did not mind it at all. It was not only that the material was new to me, but also that I found so much of it convincing and interesting. In no time at all, and largely without realising it, I was a paid-up Leavisite, although I would never have put it that way. 'Leavisian' we accepted, but 'Leavisite' was a term which those of us reading English at Downing in my time resented and disliked. In the way it was used, it suggested mindless discipleship, a blind following of the master. How unfair this was, we protested, when it was Leavis who had said that a judgement was personal or it was nothing, and who had insisted so heavily on literary criticism as an essentially collaborative venture, 'the common pursuit of true judgement' in that phrase from Eliot he had borrowed for the title of one of his most influential books. Had he not also put into circulation that model or paradigm of literary discussion in which one party says 'This is so, isn't?' while the other responds with 'Yes, but ...'? Was it likely that a teacher with these attitudes would be responsible for epigones without minds of their own? A feeble joke we enjoyed at the time concerned a young man who, asked what he thinks of Leavis, replies 'I admire him greatly but don't agree with everything he says'. This depended for its comic effect on a hidden contradiction. How could anyone who really admired and understood Leavis fail to realise that agreement or disagreement with his particular literary judgements was irrelevant to what he had to teach?

I can see now that there was a good deal of hypocrisy in our enjoyment of this story. In the numerous contacts our particular year had with Leavis, I cannot remember many examples of 'yes but' from our side; and nor was the manner in which he addressed us markedly interrogative ('this is so, isn't it?). In the early 1960s, he was nearing the end of his career. Having spent a lifetime pondering a huge variety of literary issues, he knew what he felt about most of them. It would have been hard for him to make those thoughts appear tentative, just as it was hard for us to offer meaningful qualification. That we were largely mere listeners in Leavis's seminars did not bother me but I suppose I may have been vaguely aware, even then, that in saying quite as much as he did, he was infringing one of his own principles. We were constantly reminded that a literary text is never more than black marks on a white page and only comes into real existence in the mind, the response of an individual reader. A teacher can help students towards that response but it would be an absurdity to imagine that he or she could have it for them. It may have been a recollection of this truism, allied to an unusual degree of natural shyness, which helped determine the pedagogic technique of one my Downing supervisors. We had three seminars a week with Leavis but then, in addition to these, weekly or more often fortnightly supervisions in which we were able to discuss an essay we had written with one of Leavis's former students who was doing graduate work, and held some temporary post at Downing or elsewhere in the university. For a good deal of my early time, my supervisor was John Newton who was certainly not going to fall into the trap of talking too much. He had in fact a quite remarkable power for keeping silent, pondering his own thoughts and allowing his students all the space in the world to ponder theirs. In the hour or so that my supervision would last, there was a complete absence of dominance or infringement. Before I got used to the method, I found the long silences desperately uncomfortable and unnerving: they made me feel like a sufferer from Tourette's syndrome who has accidentally stumbled into a Quaker prayer meeting. I know I was not the only person to suffer in this way. In his first novel, Howard Jacobson has reflected a little on his Cambridge education and a supervisor whom he calls Derek Muten. After describing Muten's extreme social unease before a supervision began, Jacobson goes on to say that the supervision itself was only distinguished from what went before 'by a marked increase in the level of communicated reticence and pain', and to then describe the stretches of ten or fifteen minutes in any supervision when Muten 'allowed his head to drop between his knees, and his soul, as far as one could detect the difference, to leave his body'.

Jacobson's ten or fifteen minutes is an obvious comic exaggeration (it's surprising how long even one minute of silence can seem), but he captures the atmosphere of supervisions with John Newton well. Yet I eventually came to feel that he was an excellent supervisor and that I derived a lot from his teaching. He never forgot that in literary critical discussion a teacher can show, elicit, prompt but never *tell*. I thought of him often later when I began teaching and felt myself turning into a tiresome windbag. I tried the silent treatment occasionally but it never worked and I hadn't the temperament to sustain it. I have to say in self-defence that there was a feature of the Downing model here which was, to use the jargon of the sociologists, barely operational. The interchange it proposed was between more or less equal partners but, however much cleverer than their teachers some students may be, there is usually an imbalance of power at the root of the teaching situation which can make the assumption of equality seem like a pretence. And since what makes for the difference is largely experience, the greater the age gap between student and teacher the greater that imbalance tends to be. We certainly recognised it between ourselves and Leavis who was always ready to *tell* us all kinds of things. If I didn't mind that it was because he had so many interesting things to tell and was always lively, sharp and indiscreet. Like most successful teachers, Leavis was something of a performer. He would enliven the seminars with stories from his early days in Cambridge, telling us, with an ironic twinkle in his eye, that the master of Christ's was so good looking that the local tailors would dress him for free in order to advertise their wares. He would personalise his teaching so that I can remember him holding up a copy of Nietzsche's *Birth of Tragedy* (a text he admired) and saying that he had also read it in French but even they couldn't make it entirely clear. He would observe that his ability to swim for fifty yards under water was a good training for reading Swinburne and, discussing an erotic poem by the Earl of Rochester, would clutch his solar plexus and say, 'it comes from here, you know' before adding, after a significant pause, 'or even lower'. But what Leavis struck me as being above all was endlessly indulgent to the slothful, philistine and half-educated creatures who sat before him (I speak for myself). I never heard him utter a harsh word and if he was disappointed in us, he did not let it show.

THREE

SANCTIMONIOUS PRICK?

I n the second volume of his autobiography, Stephen Fry, who went to Cambridge almost twenty years after I did, refers to Leavis as a 'sanctimonious prick of only parochial significance'. I take this to be more or less the current view, colourfully expressed; but it seems to me wrong on two counts. In the first place, the significance of Leavis in his own day was far from parochial. This was in part because he had established a power base in the schools to which my fellow students at Downing were the living testimony. From the beginning he had seen the importance of secondary education, writing with Denys Thompson a handbook for teachers called *Culture and Environment*. A diatribe against the modern 'machine age' and all that went with it, this book often appealed to the account of the decline in critical standards which Leavis's wife had provided in her *Fiction and the Reading Public*, and described various ways in which schoolchildren could be given a training in 'critical awareness' that would make them resistant to attempts by advertisers or journalists to debase their emotional lives. Thompson was himself a schoolteacher and, under the title *Reading and Discrimination*, he shortly went on to put together an anthology of passages from English literature for class use which was inspired by the Leavises and heavily reliant on their work. This was in the 1930s when Leavis was making contacts in the schools which would prove fruitful later. After a while he was able to send young men he had taught back into the system and build up an impressive network of influence, which he strengthened with the success (or notoriety) of his own publications.

Both these schoolbooks were empire building, not for its own sake but in the service of an ideal. What the ideal was can most economically be suggested by considering Leavis's concept of the English language as a transmitter of cultural value: 'At the centre of our culture is language, and while we have our language tradition is, in some essential sense, still alive'. He insisted on the belief that it is only in the work of the greatest writers that English grows and develops in a fruitful way, with beneficial effects for the quality of life of *all* its users. An elite of trained readers was essential if the growth and development manifested by the best contemporary authors was to be recognised and appreciated since, without this recognition, their efforts would fall on deaf ears and have no chance of being repeated, with correspondingly dire consequences for the culture as a whole. The situation was critical because as capitalism gained an increasingly tight grip on the collective mind, and the reading public became ever more diverse and fragmented, traditional organs of culture like the Press lowered their standards in order to appeal to a greater number of readers. It was against this general dumbing-down that Leavis hoped his pupils would fight, an embattled group maintaining continuity with what was best in the past and promoting whatever was best in the present.

From our current perspective, the cause Leavis represented must now look hopeless – 'that ship has sailed', a young person of today might have told him; but his championing of it had an effect which in its time was not merely parochial. Nor was he, in his leadership, notably sanctimonious. Certainly I never found him so. It is true that, as his enemies never tired of saying, he was a moralist and a fairly puritanical one at that. He admits as much at the beginning of *The Great Tradition* when he is mocking Lord David Cecil for suggesting that it was somehow a limitation on George Eliot that 'her standards of right and wrong were the Puritan standards. She admired truthfulness and chastity and industry and self-restraint, she disapproved of loose living and recklessness and deceit and self indulgence'. 'I had better confess', Leavis comments ironically, 'that I differ (apparently) from Lord David Cecil in sharing these beliefs, admirations, and disapprovals, so that the reader knows my bias at once'. This was indeed his bias but in my experience he was always too sharp, witty and self-aware to have anything of the holy Willy about him. Late in his life he described his amusement at finding himself referred to in an Italian newspaper as a *puritano frenetico* and reminded his listeners that, at the beginning of his career, his willingness to discuss *Ulysses* and *Lady Chatterley's Lover* with his students had incurred sufficient official disfavour for there to have been talk in an undergraduate magazine of 'the Leavis prize for pornography'.

Leavis was no prude but he was, as I say, a moralist and moral values are always going to play a part in any fully responsive reading of literature. The danger comes when our judgement of a work of art begins to hinge on our approval or otherwise of certain attitudes, however well or badly they may be represented. Signs of such a tendency can no doubt be found scattered throughout Leavis's writing (especially perhaps in his work on Lawrence), but I can remember only two hints of it in his seminars. One came when he was considering Samuel Butler's *The Way of All Flesh*, which begins with what is generally acknowledged to be a satirical portrait of its author's father. In the course of his discussion, his thoughts turned musingly to Sir Arthur Quiller-Couch, the individual in charge when the Cambridge English degree was first launched in the early 1920s. A literary journalist as well as a professor of English, Quiller-Couch was always known by his pen-name 'Q' and, although Leavis's tone in referring to him was mildly disparaging, it was also always affectionate. He had once heard 'Q' say about Butler, he reflected, that no man should ever turn on his father and I felt that this was so much his own view that he found it difficult to consider *The Way of All Flesh* objectively. I did not know then that Leavis had been particularly attached to his own father who died after a motor-cycle accident at about the same time that he himself began his final degree examinations.

The more serious hint of moral feelings over-riding critical judgement concerned Proust. One shorthand way he had of expressing his feeling about *À la recherche du temps perdu* was to say that, if he had the choice, he would rather re-read Samuel Richardson's *Clarissa* than Proust's novel, the implication being that both were stiff tasks. It is of course the case that *À la recherche* is far from being continuously interesting and that it takes a special taste to stay awake through its long and complex descriptions of natural phenomena. But what Leavis appeared to object to, as he elaborated his view, was Proust's constant preoccupation with his homosexuality and the way in which, as the novel proceeds, a surprisingly number of the characters turn out to be gay. There seemed to me at the time a suggestion of moral disapproval when Leavis mentioned this and that it was one which prevented him from appreciating to the full a social satirist as vivid and entertaining as Austen, Dickens or George Eliot, and one of the most subtle analysts of human motive in literature. It cannot, I suppose, have helped that Proust was a major figure in the value system of his enemies in King's College and in Bloomsbury.

The charge that Leavis was too much of a moralist is usually accompanied by the complaint that he was narrow and exclusive, which is strange given that in his own writing his range is much wider than that of most other academic critics. John Carey voiced it once in an interview with Clive James, citing, as people always do, the passage at the beginning of *The Great Tradition* where Leavis claims that Fielding is not one of the truly great novelists and then goes on: 'He is important not because he leads to Mr. J. B. Priestley but because he leads to Jane Austen, to appreciate whose distinction is to feel that life isn't long enough to permit of one's giving much time to Fielding or any to Mr. Priestley'. This is characteristic of the way Leavis tends to see the history of English literature in terms of Crewe Junction, one main line leading to another; but also in its dismissive clearing of the ground. The tone was not one he developed as he grew in confidence and reputation but had had from the beginning. In the first chapter of *New Bearings in English Poetry*, for example, where he is describing that withdrawal from active everyday life into a dream world so characteristic of much late Victorian writing, he denies that Browning constitutes a significant exception. 'There are kinds of strength a poet is best without', he observes and declares that 'Browning would have been less robust if he had been more sensitive and intelligent'. Warming to his theme, he then adds that 'it is possible to consider [Browning] as a philosophical or psychological poet only by confusing intelligence with delight in the exercise of certain grosser cerebral muscles'. Lovers of Browning cannot have found it pleasant to read this kind of thing, but the no-nonsense manner was appealing to young people so that one major danger of being at Downing was of trying to imitate it, and taking over, in the process, judgements one had not remotely earned. I can remember going home one vacation and visiting three Welsh teachers, a couple and their female friend, who were a model of devoted service to the community and had been very kind to me when they lived next door to us in Pendlebury. The man was an unusually mild, gentle individual who, as I was expounding the history of English poetry, timidly suggested that he had always found Browning rewarding. I hope and believe that I did not openly reproach him for his bad taste, but I have a distinct sense that I made him feel he was behind the times, even though my own knowledge of Browning's verse was minimal in comparison with his. Leavis was not himself a sanctimonious prick, but he may have had a tendency to produce them.

Having clear ideas of literary value was what was known in the Leavis group as discrimination. This was a key concept when I was at Downing, so much so that one of my fellow students used to sing a song of his own composition which began, 'I met Dr Leavis the other day and when I went up to him this is what he did say, "Dis-CRIM-in-A-shun is life"', and so on in that calypso rhythm so popular in those years. One of the things I think Leavis meant by saying that discrimination is life was that it is an instinctive habit woven into all our activities (no-one objects to the selectors of a football team discriminating). He would illustrate this truth by quoting a passage from Robert Graves's *Goodbye to All That* which I afterwards discovered he had used as one of the epigraphs to *The Common Pursuit*. This occurs when Graves describes how, at the end of his first term at Oxford, one of the dons in his college said to him a little stiffly, 'I understand, Mr. Graves, that the essays you write for your English tutor are, shall I say, a trifle temperamental. It appears, indeed, that you prefer some authors to others.' We thought of this as comic in the way 'I admire Dr Leavis greatly but don't agree with everything he says' was comic, and we had our own, demotic version in the story of a teacher from another college who says to his student in a supervision, 'Let me stop you there, Alistair. You were just about to make a value judgement and we don't come on to value judgements until next term'.

The discriminations we were encouraged to practise, or which Leavis practised for us, reduced English literature to manageable proportions but friends have sometimes asked me whether I did not therefore find my education unreasonably restricted. I cannot honestly say that I did. In my penultimate year at school I won what was called 'the English prize' and was asked to choose a book which could be handed to me on the platform. My choice was the complete plays of Oscar Wilde. I cannot recall looking at these once while I was at Downing, or for many years after. Only quite recently, when I had to teach a course on comedy, did I read again *The Importance of Being Ernest* and rediscover what a great work of art it is. But Wilde was not the kind of figure who was easily accommodated in Leavisian terms. In *The Great Tradition* he makes clear that the authors who interest him have 'a vital capacity for experience, a kind of reverent openness before life, and a marked moral intensity', while he dismisses Arnold Bennett from serious consideration on the grounds that he never seems 'to have been disturbed enough about life'. Whether or not Wilde was seriously disturbed by life, 'marked moral intensity' is not a phrase which it is easy to associate with him. In an account of Leavis which is in large part favourable, Lionel Trilling once complained that he did not take proper account 'of the art that delights – and enlightens – by intentional relaxation of moral awareness, by its invitation to us to contemplate the mere excess of irrelevant life', and he added that there was not enough consideration in Leavis's work of 'the impulse of sheer *performance*, even of virtuosity, which, whether we respond to it in acrobatics or in athletics or in prestidigitation or in the ballet or in music or in literature, is of enormous value'. Quite what value this impulse has, and how the critic is to talk about it, are matters Trilling does not make clear; but his remarks seem to point in the right direction and help explain what is generally recognised as the major misjudgement Leavis made when, in his initial account of the great tradition of English novelists, he excluded Dickens.

If that exclusion gave particular succour to his enemies, it was because he later reneged on it. But the case is more complicated than they usually make out. It is quite true that in *The Great Tradition* Leavis describes Dickens as a 'great entertainer' who had for the most part 'no profounder responsibility as a creative artist than this description suggests'; and that he went on to add: 'the adult mind doesn't as a rule find in Dickens a challenge to unusual and sustained seriousness'. But this is in a context where he is describing the limitations of all the important nineteenth-century novelists: identifying the adolescent yearning which makes itself felt in even George Eliot's later work, noting how Henry James's life-style can be associated with the hypertrophy which affects his late writing, or criticising Conrad for his 'adjectival insistence'. The greatest of writers, he makes clear in an impressively sustained exercise in discrimination, have their strengths and weaknesses and although when he detects the influence of Dickens on Eliot, James and Conrad, it is usually in the spirit suggested by his descrip- tion of Conrad's *The Secret Agent* as redolent of 'a Dickens qualified by a quite un-Dickensian maturity', the long note on *Hard Times* which he appends to his book redresses the balance quite considerably. There he points out that Shakespeare was also a 'great entertainer' and says: 'The final stress may fall on Dickens's command of word, phrase, rhythm and image; in ease and range there is surely no greater master of English except Shakespeare. This comes back to saying that Dickens is a great poet'. These words pointed the way forward to the development of his views on Dickens and his later celebration of *Dombey and Son* and *Little Dorrit* as classics of English literature.

There were no doubt several authors of whom I was notionally deprived because of Leavis's Puritanism, although by the time I came to Downing Dickens was not one of them and very much back in favour. We were taught what became known as the canon, as he had defined it. Yet this was, as it happens, much the same list of writers whom hundreds of other critics, both before and during his time, had decided were worth reading. The fact that he had attacked what he felt was the excessive veneration of Milton, or written rude things about Shelley, did not mean that he felt they ought not to be studied. There was in any case quite enough in this canon for us to be getting on with. To declare that students ought to be allowed to read whatever inter- ests them, as Carey does, always makes the speaker look good since most of us are no more against free choice than we are against world peace. But in a degree that lasts only three years there is a limited amount of time and there will always therefore be a battle as to what should or should not be on the curriculum. Not everything can be taught. If one is determined to hang on to some element of compulsion, on the grounds that an English degree which has not included (for example) any poetry, anything from the eighteenth century, or any drama, ought to be called something else, then an element of discrimination has to come into play.

Compulsion has become increasingly less a feature of English degrees recently, retreating in favour of customer choice and 'options'. Whether or not this is a healthy tendency, there is a sense (very indirect and oblique) in which Leavis can be held partly responsible for it. He had been profoundly influenced at the start of his career by a number of T. S. Eliot's essays. One of these is 'Tradition and the Individual Talent' and puts forward the apparently simple idea that the literary canon is not something fixed in time but altered every time an important new work appears. 'The existing order is complete before the new work appears', Eliot writes, 'for order to persist after the supervention of novelty, the *whole* existing order must be, if ever so slightly altered; and so the relations, proportions, values of each work of art toward the whole are readjusted'. Leavis adapted this notion to criticism, insisting that the canon of great works could not be merely inherited but had always to be re-constituted from the perspective of the present. 'What mankind have long possessed they have often examined and compared, and if they persist to value the possession, it is because frequent comparisons have confirmed opinion in its favour', says Dr Johnson. But for Leavis what mattered was how the interest and value of certain literary works must inevitably change in the light of the preoccupations of the here and now. What counts in one age does not necessarily count in another. For the authority of habit or custom he attempted to substitute one based on the criteria elaborated in his own numerous readings of poems, novels and plays. His hope was that these would appeal to a number of qualified readers sufficient to provide that consensus without which literary judgement has no force. Yet in taking this course he was relativising literary judgement and therefore leaving himself open to the charge that his own choices and readings were only those of a white male of a certain class and location, and that a female reader, or one not born in this country, might want very different ones. For both those parties Leavis's choices might well seem to represent discrimination in a quite different sense from the one in which he used the word. He was right to insist that the best literary judgements come from critics who are fully alive to the state of the society in which they live; but the extent to which the world he lived in has changed since his time might be suggested by the fact that, were the publication of Thompson's *Reading and Discrimination* to be announced now, the general public would completely misunderstand what it was about.

FOUR

CLOSE READING

L eavis was, as I have said, an indulgent teacher, but then he needed to be. As he looked round his latest recruits in the fight against low standards, he must sometimes have felt like a desperate German general in the last days of the Second World War. Many of his seminars were surveys of the main figures in various set periods of English literature, but there were also sessions of what is usually known as 'practical criticism'. Because this is a term which in a few years is likely to become incomprehensible, it may be worth recording that it derives from the title of a book published in 1929 by I. A. Richards, one of the founders of the Cambridge English degree and at that time a potent influence on Leavis. Richards had had the idea of distributing to his students, and a few colleagues, a number of short poems and then asking them to write analytical commentaries that made clear which they preferred and why. Crucial was that the authorship of these poems was kept secret. The results constituted the bulk of his book and were meant to 'prepare the way for educational methods more efficient than those we use now in developing discrimination and the power to understand what we hear and read.'

Downing men had a reputation for being adept at practical criticism. They had, after all, a fine model in Leavis himself, who was a particularly gifted close reader of poetry, able to identify with a conviction that was often devastating loose rhythms, stale diction and conventionalities of feeling; but also to make his readers aware of subtleties and refinements in a good poem they had not noticed before, and thereby raise them up (if only momentarily) to his own level of sensitive awareness. The complaint often voiced against practical criticism as either a pedagogic method or an approach to reading was that it was only appropriate when the poems were indeed short (because then the whole of a work's linguistic organisation was there before you), and not therefore much use with longer ones, or with novels and plays. There was always some truth in this charge but, as far as drama was concerned, Leavis countered it by suggesting that in a play by Shakespeare (for example) there is a degree of poetic organisation which means that close investigation of one part is a clue to the whole. 'Shakespeare's marvellous faculty of intense local realization', he wrote in an early number of *Scrutiny*, 'is a faculty of realizing the whole locally'. He made efforts to carry this principle of organic unity into the study of novels where it was more difficult to apply (one reason for his initial hesitations about Dickens's novels was that they were so patently full of what he at first regarded as redundant life). When he quotes from his preferred authors in *The Great Tradition* however, and he quotes a lot, it is not so much so that he can then analyse 'local realization' but rather in order to illustrate, in what are often impressively penetrating and subtle ways, the various themes of a particular novel and the means its author is employing to convey them. What one might call the quality of the writing is something which he assumes readers can see for themselves and which it does not need practical criticism to bring out. Any other assumption would have caused him a difficult and perhaps insoluble problem of critical method – how do you keep commentary on a novel within reasonable bounds? – but I used to wonder about it when I was teaching and had to read essay after essay on a novel or play which could just have easily have been written about a short synopsis or plot summary of the work in question.

By the time of my first year with Leavis, his sheets of anonymous texts for analysis and dating included quite a lot of prose. Very early on, I can remember being confronted with a passage of what seemed to me lively polemical writing. After some analysis of its qualities, he asked us to suggest who might have been its author. To this day I have no idea how I managed to come up with the name of Cobbett or in what context I had stumbled upon the *Rural Rides*, which is still the only text of his I have ever read. Yes, said Leavis, after some hesitation, I can see why you *might* think that, and he went on to talk at some length about colloquial vigour before revealing that the author of the passage in question was Thomas Nashe. Nashe's best known work appeared in 1592 and *Rural Rides* was published in 1830 so that, if I had been looking for comfort, I could have said that, as far as dating was concerned, I was only 238 years out.

One method I have for dividing people is to imagine that there are those who, as they look back on their life, remember it chiefly in terms of the happy moments when they were congratulated, received an award, or said some something to which the response was peculiarly gratifying. Set against these are those whose progress is remembered as a series of humiliating self-exposures, occasions when they did or said the wrong thing. As an instance of saying the wrong thing in a public context, my 'Cobbett' must rank pretty high. There is a story told by Stanley Cavell about the time he attended the music theory class given by Ernst Bloch at Berkeley. Bloch would apparently play a piece by Bach, 'with one note altered by a half a step from Bach's rendering', and then play the piece as it was written. After repeating this process, he would challenge the students to hear the difference, tell them that if they could not hear it they could not call themselves musicians, and then remind them that there were after all many 'honourable trades. Shoe-making, for example.' It would have been reasonable of Leavis to suggest that anyone who could not tell the difference between Cobbett and Nashe ought to be thinking of something other than the study of English litera-ture. The enormity of my mistake became more painful with the passage of time as I gained more familiarity with Elizabethan prose writing, its often strange vocabulary and loose grammatical structures trailing off God knows where. The consolation was that at the time I made the error I had no idea how serious it was. There is another consolation which comes from those Proustian moments when a word pronounced in a special way, a chance glimpse of certain features, or the atmosphere in a room suddenly brings back an episode when we behaved in a particularly foolish manner. It strikes me then that the number of humiliating episodes which we remember, and which constitute our private store of psychological pain or discomfort, is as nothing compared to those we have either forgotten or were not even aware of at the time, and that Nature can sometimes be kind after all.

The way Leavis dealt with my mistake was a model for me later when I had to respond to similarly foolish suggestions. The technique is no doubt common as well as considerate, but I once witnessed an uncomfortable *reductio* of it at a lecture by Mason, whose Oxford classics degree was often adduced as the reason for his being the most urbane of all the Leavisites. At the lecture was someone from my year who had suffered a breakdown and whose behaviour had become mildly psychotic. When Mason had finished speaking he was asked by this student a whole series of increasingly mad questions to each of which he replied with the usual 'I can see why you might say that', 'that would be one way of looking at it' etc. until every other member of the audience was in an agony of embarrassment and silently begging him to cut their pain short with, 'No, I'm afraid what you have just said is complete rubbish'.

I don't think this is what I would have liked Leavis to have said to me. That I had spoken at all in the seminar may have been because I was aware that he was frustrated by how little effort we appeared to be making to stop it turning into a monologue. As a group, we were very often tongue-tied. This was understandable given the prestige Leavis enjoyed and the strength of his personality but at Downing there were special, additional reasons for inducing that state. 'Eupeptic' was a word Leavis would use in conversations about Robert Browning, one that was given special force by his own digestive difficulties. What it indicated was the same quality in Browning's verse he had hinted at when he wrote that if the poet had been less robust he might have been more sensitive and intelligent. It was hard not to extend this judgement from the verse to the man and, for all his awareness of the difficulty of making this transition, Leavis often wrote as if fine, sensitive writing must be the product of fine, sensitive people (and vice-versa). This is a case, he says, at the conclusion of an especially impressive close reading of Hardy's *After a Journey*, 'in which we know from the art what the man was like; we can be sure, that is, what personal qualities we should have found to admire in Hardy if we could have known him'.

But if one could tell what someone was like from their poetry, might not that also be true of their literary criticism? A sentence in the 'manifesto' which appeared in the first number of *Scrutiny* refers chillingly to 'a necessary relationship between the quality of an individual's response to the arts and his general fitness for a humane existence'. Although it was not a deliberate policy, there is no doubt that when we were asked by Leavis and our supervisors to respond to certain books, our fitness for a humane existence always seemed to be on the line. The effect was inhibiting, and extended to what we wrote. The supervisors at Downing were good at taking an essay and exposing just the kind of reliance on cliché and shallow feeling Leavis might excoriate in a bad poem. For some of us, the effects of this general atmosphere and training were long-lasting, and it was not until middle age slackened the sinews, and certain precepts faded from the memory, that we began to put pen to paper with any regularity.

When we looked at lines of poetry, or passages in a novel, it was as if our very lives depended on it, and so in a way they did. Personal response to literature was after all what mattered and there were none of the escapes an English degree now offers, and did then, from a struggle with the text. In all the essays I wrote at Cambridge, for example, I cannot recall ever providing a footnote, and there certainly seemed a relative indifference among my teachers to the edition I was using, the historical context of the text I was reading, what critics in the past had made of it, and in general anything which might be filed under the heading of literary scholarship. This fact associates itself in my mind with my absence from the majority of Faculty lectures. In Cambridge students were taught in their colleges, as no doubt they still are, by people who may or may not have been appointed members of an over-arching, centralising English Faculty. It was a matter of bitter resentment for Leavis that he was given the financial security of a Faculty post much later than most of his less gifted but more clubbable contemporaries, and that he was never promoted to a chair. The Faculty was responsible for the setting and marking of examinations as well as the provision of lecture series tied into those examinations. Some quite well known figures were lecturing in the Faculty in the early 1960s, including (for example) C. S. Lewis. I cannot say Leavis specifically told us not to attend these lectures, but he made it pretty plain that we could find better ways of using our time. Spending the morning in the lecture halls could after all only be a distraction from our chief job of coming to terms with whatever difficult text we happened to be reading that week, learning how to tune into its distinctive idioms so that we could engage in meaningful critical discussion. Concentrating as we did on reading and sometimes re-reading a particular text, we were like nothing so much as the early Protestants let loose for the first time on the translated Bible and struggling to work out its meanings, regardless of Church authority.

I realise there must be some distortion in my memory here. No-one who picks up a book is a complete *tabula rasa*. I must have already known a good deal about the authors I studied; I certainly read introductions, and Shakespeare in annotated editions. The occasional critical book doubtless crossed my path and I had three weekly seminars with Leavis to provide a context for my reading. But of the general spirit in Downing I am pretty certain. Why else, since I normally have such a poor memory for verse, have I always been able to quote at will Pope's couplet:

> The bookful blockhead, ignorantly read
> With loads of learned lumber in his head.

One of the more entertaining ways Leavis had of keeping us interested was to demonstrate the irrelevance of many of the notes in an Arden edition of Shakespeare, how they lay inert on the page without any power to inflect reading, to produce what Wittgenstein calls 'aspect change'. We all somehow knew also that, when he had reviewed a volume of the Twickenham Pope, he had confessed to the inevitable revulsion he felt at seeing *The Dunciad* trickle 'thinly through a desert of apparatus, to disappear time and again from sight'. But what best expressed the Downing attitude to scholarship for me was a passage from Arnold's 'On Translating Homer' where Arnold is defending himself against the charge of being insufficiently informed:

MEMOIRS OF A LEAVISITE

Alas! that is very true. Much as Mr Newman was mistaken when he talked of my rancour, he is entirely right when the talks of my ignorance. And yet, perverse as it seems to say so, I sometime find myself wishing, when dealing with these matters of poetical criticism, that my ignorance were even greater than it is. To handle these matters properly there is needed a poise so perfect that the least overweight in any direction tends to destroy the balance. Temper destroys it, a crochet destroys it, even erudition may destroy it. ... The late Duke of Wellington said of a certain peer that "it was a great pity his education had been so far too much for his abilities". In like manner, one often sees erudition out of all proportion to its owner's critical faculty. Little as I know, therefore, I am always apprehensive, in dealing with poetry, lest even that little should prove "too much for my abilities".

I am not certain Leavis would have been entirely comfortable with the tone of these remarks. He was fond of quoting with approval Gerald Manley Hopkins's rebuke to Robert Bridges for calling Arnold 'Mr Kid-Glove Cocksure'; but there was perhaps a little too much that was smooth and polished in the Arnoldian manner for his taste. Yet of the general position adumbrated here, I am sure he would have approved.

The way I would now describe the Downing attitude to scholarship would be to say that we asked ourselves, 'what is the least I need to know in order to read this text intelligently?' But that begs the essential question. The trouble with information is that there is no way of knowing how it will bear on a fully responsive reading until one has become aware of it. This is the dilemma which licenses an endless production of data, most of which will lie inert but some of which might well prove crucial. It is a question therefore of taking risks and we much preferred the danger of being betrayed by our ignorance to that of substituting close familiarity with a text for information about it. From a pedagogic point of view, what strikes me most about this attitude in retrospect is that it was no more easily 'operational' than the assumption of equality between teacher and students in the Leavisian model of critical discussion. The simplest way to distinguish university teachers from their students is to say that the former know more than the latter, and the simplest way to define a lecture is to say that it consists in a transmission of knowledge from one party to another. This is no doubt a crudely distorting account of what actually happens in subjects like history or the social sciences, but it is one to which both the general public and many university authorities are wedded. For Leavisian teachers of English however, much of what the student needs to know about a text will be implicit in the text itself and they will be chary of communicating additional information in case it should prove not only irrelevant but distracting. 'For the purposes of criticism', Leavis writes in the first essay in *The Common Pursuit*, 'scholarship, unless directed by an intelligent interest in poetry – without, that is, critical sensibility and the skill that enables the critic to develop its responses in sensitive and closely relevant thinking – is useless'. But it is difficult to explain to the outside world that although bibliographical, historical and social details may sometimes be very important, it is not as a scholar one takes one's stand.

To say to a vice-chancellor that one's primary concern is to provide an environment in which students are encouraged to read with care and attention a number of often difficult books has never put the head of an English department in a strong position. This is in spite of the fact that attentive reading is a far from easy affair. Finding out which parts of a novel, play or poem have been responsible for our total response, whether there are elements in that response that are merely idiosyncratic, what the right words might be to express our feelings, or how we meet the challenge of someone who has read the text as carefully as we have – all these processes in the phenomenology of reading, and many more besides (including those which relate to questions of value), can be arduous. They might seem to require a degree of self-understanding, linguistic skill and indeed *precisely invoked* knowledge which justifies the centrality Leavis gave to reading in his conception of English as a university discipline. In his frequent accounts of how in the 1920s the Cambridge English degree came into being, he always had high praise for Henry Chadwick, the professor of Anglo-Saxon at the time, who insisted that his own subject should not be one of the new degree's compulsory components. Whereas those who designed the English course in Oxford appeared to have felt that the subject would degenerate into a soft option unless it could be bolstered with disciplines which were more obviously labour-intensive, for Leavis and his colleagues in Cambridge, it was already hard enough. They were aware that a genuinely serious discussion of the strengths, weaknesses and value of works like *Antony and Cleopatra*, *The Rape of the Lock*, *The Prelude* or *Dombey and Son* can indeed leave one exhausted. I become conscious of the truth of this when I accidently stumble into one and realise how recent developments in the university have played havoc with all the necessary muscles. With colleagues so often preoccupied with their own specialities, there is less opportunity than there used to be for an exchange of views and the notion that there could ever be some 'ideal reading' towards which a number of people might feel they were striving has long been discredited. It sometimes seems to me therefore that, with the proliferation of amateur reading groups, there is more literary criticism outside the university than in it, although in its less rigorous forms the activity is so instinctive that this view may be unnecessarily pessimistic. All

I would want to affirm therefore is that it would always have been difficult to maintain its central importance in a university environment. Asked what it is that they do, those English teachers who reply literary criticism are likely to be told that in this they are no different from everyone else in the department and then be required to specify what else it is they can offer.

FIVE

TIME OUT

A university is, or ought to be, a world of extraordinary new possibilities for the student who first arrives there. I was one of the gullible horde who signed up for the freshmen's tour of the Cambridge Union, forked out the rather large joining fee, and never set foot in the building again. But for those not interested in trying to make their way into politics, there were plenty of other ways of spending their spare time: societies of all sorts that catered for a myriad of interests. A fair number of students always regarded this extra-curricular life as the one for which they had come to university in the first place, treating their academic work as a necessary excuse for pursuing what really mattered to them. Stephen Fry describes himself as one of these but for me a more relevant, if much earlier example here would be T. C. Worsley, the author of that splendid memoir which takes its title from a reference to 'flannelled fools at the wicket' in a Kipling poem. After having been a public school teacher for a while, Worsley spent most of his life writing drama criticism for the *New Statesmen* and the *Financial Times*. In his last year at Cambridge, which must still have been in the 1920s, he was taught by Leavis whom he describes as arriving at the supervision 'dressed in an open shirt which shocked us to the depth of our conventional souls, his bald head brown with nature culture'. That he found Leavis stimulating and remained an admirer long after he had left university did not mean that he did much work there, and he confesses to having spent most of his time either on the playing field or in 'The Hawks Club smoking room', where all the serious Cambridge sportsmen congregated.

As a schoolboy, a lot of my time was spent in sporting activities. I liked soccer without being much good at it. After I had left school and was waiting to go to university, I went to the trouble of joining Sale rugby club and played a few games at scrum half for the most minor of their teams. Having never even watched rugby union – it was my enthusiasm for the league variety that sent me to Sale – and never having played it, I was understandably incompetent. I played neither soccer nor rugby well, but was always quite good at cricket. My father had built an asbestos garage by the side of our house and I hung a ball on a string from the roof so that I could spend hours prodding forward, perfecting my forward defensive stroke. It was unfortunate that during that time I developed a habit of holding the bat in a way which made it easy for me to cut and pull, but never allowed me to drive with any ease or grace. My eye was nevertheless sharp enough to have me marked out as a promising wicket keeper/batsman and, when I was fifteen, I was playing for Swinton in the Lancashire and Cheshire League. For people outside the county, any mention of the Lancashire leagues tends to suggest teams which had once had cricketers like Constantine or Sobers playing for them. Swinton did have a professional, although he must have been paid precious little. He was a minor figure who may have represented his island in the West Indies but had, I am pretty sure, never figured in a test match. He did however have famous friends and, when his benefit match came along, I found myself keeping wicket behind Conrad Hunte who opened for the West Indies on over forty occasions and finished with an average of 46. I say I was keeping wicket but I don't think the ball ever came through to me and I was particularly impressed when, after Hunte had scored about 90, our man said to him 'That will do Conrad'. The very next ball he holed out to long-on with startling precision.

Being an enthusiastic soccer player, and a competent cricketer, made life easy for me at school, where these two sports were highly regarded. They carried a deal of kudos and Howard Jacobson has justifiably complained of how, at morning assembly, the headmaster would announce details of our cricket scores against the local grammar schools while the fact that he was playing table tennis for the county went unregarded. But I was never going to be good enough at cricket to play for Cambridge and was never therefore in danger of wasting my time in the Hawks smoking room since that club was largely reserved for blues (although Worsley was not one). In my first year at Downing I did play for the college team and spent an entertaining two weeks during the summer in a tour of British army bases in Germany where I drank a lot, scored some runs, and caught a few catches (if I stumped anyone, I have forgotten it). But when I began my second year I dropped sport altogether and did not play cricket again for fifteen or so years by which time any promise I had previously possessed was long gone.

Once I became focussed on trying to make something of my university studies, and was infused with a Leavisian sense of the social importance of literary criticism, there seemed no time for sports. The general atmosphere at Downing appeared in any case to be against them, despite the fact that John Newton had boxed for the university and Leavis himself always cut an athletic figure. It was said that he had been an effective wing forward at school, a possibility hard to believe given his size and the behemoths who now play in that position; but he was no doubt aggressive enough. Someone who was at Downing in the 1950s recalls organising a meeting which he feared might be disrupted by the boat club. When Leavis got wind of this threat he apparently offered to attend on the grounds that 'I can be pretty handy in a roughhouse'. Hard as it is to visualise this man of about five foot six, who can never have weighed much more than nine stone, sorting out a group of young oarsmen, the remark shows the same spirit that caused him never to avoid controversy in his writing. Perhaps then he was indeed a good rugby player at school, but the sport he practised most in his later years was running. Even in old age his stamina was prodigious and running was how he worked off his enormous store of nervous energy and kept himself fit. But that is not a real sport, more of an exercise, so that the general disapproval of team games as childish and regressive which I sensed at Downing, was hardly mitigated by his example. They are no doubt both those things, but I liked the camaraderie of being in a team and I used to feel later that there were many less harmless ways of wasting your time.

From the end of my first year at Cambridge I concentrated on reading books, although not with the examinations in mind. By the early 1960s Leavis was so seriously alienated from the English Faculty that, to the limited extent the examination structure it imposed made possible, he liked to pursue his own agenda. He therefore made reading English at Downing feel like an autonomous activity which was on occasions rudely interrupted by inappropriate testing from outside. The only advice I can recall him giving about examination technique was to the effect that it was important to keep a damp handkerchief in the pocket because, covering page after page at top speed in summer, could make the hand sweaty. This was a period still dominated by the three hour stand-and-deliver paper, which he detested and often complained about. Those who did well in that exercise he could not help regarding with some suspicion. His description of Browning as 'eupeptic' was an illustration of his occasional fondness for an unusual word, and his term for a competent examinee was 'sciolist'. The fluency of sciolists must be regarded with distrust in his view. More generally, since the powers who ran the academic and intellectual world were so blind to what might constitute real standards, how could success in it be anything other than suspect?

It is not hard to see how an analysis of that world which he was able to make convincing in so many ways, could easily become, at our lower level, a convenient excuse for failure.

The primary object of my reading was self-improvement, a task for which it was unreasonable of me to expect books to take all the responsibility. That there were other cultural opportunities available is evident from the fact that the actor Joe Melia, who provides the links in Richard Attenborough's film version of 'Oh, what a lovely war!' and had a successful career as an actor, was only a couple of years ahead of me at Downing; and that Trevor Nunn, who became a director of both the Royal Shakespeare Company and the National Theatre, was in my year. But I had no taste or ability for the stage and neither, as far as I am aware, had Leavis. He went to the occasional amateur performances of Shakespeare plays put on by the colleges in summer, but never talked of having been to see a performance in London. In his criticism of Shakespeare he ignored the approach which was later to become so popular, thanks partly to his former Girton pupil Muriel Bradbrook, and which has provided such a rich mine of doctorates, chairs and institutes in recent times. The fact that Shakespeare originally wrote for the stage was of marginal interest to him, as were the conditions of the Elizabethan and Jacobean theatre. The organic unity he found in the plays was that of a dramatic poem and it was in details of imagery and rhythm that he found the key to Shakespeare's extraordinary insight into human affairs. I doubt that many actors could have spoken the lines he analysed so acutely in a way that satisfied him. He had an unusually sharp ear for anything that felt like posturing and would often give comic imitations of what he felt was a vein of Irish theatricality in some of Yeats's writing. But a degree of theatricality necessarily accompanies most acting and, in any case, he was interested in complexities of linguistic organisation in Shakespeare which may well have been difficult to convey and which were likely to remain hidden to the average playgoer who only heard them spoken.

All this might have meant that he inclined away from the theatre to the cinema, where celluloid provided a distance which protects the onlooker from being too much imposed upon by another live human being; but for Leavis, film was a medium too much a product of modern industrial civilisation. Although some film criticism did appear in the early numbers of *Scrutiny*, he tended to regard the cinema as just one more of those passive entertainments which were ruining the nation's social life (this was before day-time television), and more a tool of capitalist propaganda than an art form. That Wittgenstein could often be found in the queue outside a local Cambridge cinema waiting to see whatever happened to be showing, both baffled and amused him. When you are doing philosophy all day, he would explain to us with a wry smile, you perhaps need a period of complete mindlessness in order to recover. He was similarly indulgent towards one of his closest collaborators, D. W. Harding, who (like many academics) relaxed by reading detective stories. Yet the concept of abandoning the mind to a form of art you knew to be inferior, what might colloquially be described as intellectual slumming, puzzled him. When I am too tired to do any real work, he once explained to a friend, I listen to a record or read something I admire but have read before.

Neither theatre nor cinema formed a part of my informal education at Downing, but music was a different matter. Although I never heard Leavis discuss any particular composer, I learnt later that his father had been a competent violinist, that one of his sons was a brilliant musician, and that he himself had a stack of favourite classical recordings. The person who introduced me to music was not however Leavis but another of my Cambridge supervisors, Morris Shapira. He had a huge collection of records, as well as the latest equipment, and was the first person I had known who not only listened to classical music fairly continuously but would buy different recordings of the same piece in order to compare them. In those days the music of Berlioz was being re-discovered and I can remember reporting to him that someone I knew had pronounced the *Symphonie Fantastique*, or more likely a particular recording of it, vulgar. After pausing a little, Shapira said he thought this was perhaps right. I felt then as an outsider might over-hearing two Japanese women discussing how a colleague had performed the tea ceremony. Unfamiliar as I was with classical music, I did slowly develop a liking for it although the taste I settled into seems to me now, as I look back, essentially that of someone with no musical background and a non-musical nature. I have always preferred, for example, single instruments – Bach's unaccompanied violin and cello pieces in particular – or trios and quartets to more complicated orchestral music. Perhaps more revealing is that at the centre of my interest is opera, with its strong literary component. That meant above all Mozart, but then the composers who came after him: the Cimarosa whom Stendhal so admired (I can remember going to considerable lengths to procure *The Secret Marriage* because he rated it as highly as *The Marriage of Figaro*), but also Donizetti and then Rossini. Since I always needed cheering up, I loved the lightness and fun in their work although I was aware that it did not often bear too much investigation. An indication of how limited my taste was, according to the prevailing standards of that time (as well as of most others), is that although I tried to follow Shapira in believing that Verdi's music became more interesting in his later years, I always found that, rather than come to terms with *Falstaff* or *Otello*, I would much rather listen again to *La Traviata*.

The supervision method of Shapira was not at all like Newton's. Eliot says that the literary critic has only two tools, analysis and comparison, and if that is the case, Shapira was very strong on the latter. He was a master of suggestion, often not answering directly a point I had been trying to make in an essay but reading out a passage from the text we were studying, or something quite other, and inviting me to think about its implications. I can remember an essay I wrote for him on Burns in which I poured my heart out in an effort to explain why I thought *Tam O'Shanter* a masterpiece (a belief I still hold) and Burns himself, in spite of all the linguistic difficulties with which he presents an English reader, one of the greatest poets who ever lived. It went down well enough I think but instead of trying to qualify what I had to say and curb my enthusiasm, Shapira spent much of the supervision reading out passages from Pope which were roughly analogous in content to those from Burns that I had quoted. His intention, as I understood it, was clearly not to do Burns down, but simply to broaden my own emotional range by contrasting his populism with what was metropolitan and urbane. The effect was strengthened by the evidence all around me of his own sophisticated tastes. In those days, most supervisions took place in the teachers' rooms, flats or houses. Shapira came from a wealthy family and could afford expensive furnishing and decoration in a strikingly avant-garde style. There was a good deal of art work on the walls, he himself wore colourful clothes, and was very interested in cooking. I found the contrast he offered with Leavis, who was notably austere in his dress and habits, and who appeared to me to have only a moderate interest in art, educational. The two of them usefully complemented each other and Shapira showed that critical rigour and a luxurious, even sybaritic way of life were not always mutually exclusive. The respect that Leavis clearly had for him, before the unfortunate affair of the F. R. Leavis Lectureship, also indicated that his supposed narrowness did not extend to failing to get on with people who in their way of life were quite different from himself.

Once I had stopped playing cricket, there was nothing much I did at Cambridge outside literature apart from listening to a little music. A friend of mine revealed recently that he had become president of the Cambridge film society while he was studying modern languages and I know that another, who read history, was in his student days already making a name for himself as an expert in modern art. Both of them were public schoolboys and must therefore have found it easier to settle in at Cambridge than I did. Stephen Fry describes well, not only the advantage of having often been separated from his family before he went to Cambridge, but also how familiar the routine of college life was to him after public school (although he also says the same about the three months he spent in prison on remand after a credit card fraud). I am not sure, however, that this has much relevance in my case. There was no doubt a constitutional lack of enterprise but also the feeling that I needed all the time available in order to try to make myself worthy of participation in a noble cause. These, we were made to understand, were the cultural Dark Ages: you had only to look at the *Times Literary Supplement* or the Sunday broadsheets to be sure. On his first return to London from Mexico in 1923, D. H. Lawrence compared the state of British culture to that of Christianity after the collapse of the Roman Empire, finding some reason to hope in a memory of the monasteries. 'In the howling wilderness of slaughter and débâcle,' he writes, 'tiny monasteries of monks too obscure and poor to plunder, kept the eternal light of man's undying effort of consciousness alive.' Sometimes we deluded ourselves into thinking that we were like these monks trying to keep alive, not so much 'the eternal light of man's undying effort of consciousness' but, rather more soberly, the ability to distinguish good writing from bad.

SIX

QDL

Irreverently and chauvinistically, Mrs Leavis was usually referred to by our group as Queenie. In spite of the Q. D. Leavis which appeared on her books (the D standing for Dorothy), I thought for years that this involved an abbreviation or sobriquet of some kind. Only much later did I come across John Osborne's references to his Aunt Queenie and realise that the name was one actually given to some girls by their parents around the beginning of the last century. Much as I enjoyed being taught by her husband, I cannot say the same for her. She had been very ill when I first arrived at Downing and had been forced to go through several gruelling operations, followed by even more gruelling treatments, so that she only reappeared as a supervisor in my last year. I was sent to her along with a fellow student in my group called John Wiltshire, the author subsequently of excellent books on Dr Johnson and Jane Austen. I assume the topic was nineteenth-century fiction, since that was her speciality, but I cannot remember anything at all about the supervisions beyond the fact that Mrs Leavis was dissatisfied with our performance. The reason I know this is that one of the other supervisors casually remarked one day that she felt Wiltshire and I corresponded closely to Sir James Chetham, as he is described in the second chapter of *Middlemarch*. This was a novel we all knew well so that I had no difficulty in going to the exact sentences she clearly had in mind. They are quoted by Leavis in *The Great Tradition* and occur when Sir James is contemplating marriage to Dorothea, even though she is a girl who is clearly much cleverer than he is:

he felt himself to be in love in the right place, and was able to endure a great deal of predominance, which, after all, a man could always put down when he liked. Sir James had no idea he should ever like to put down the predominance of this handsome girl, in whose cleverness he delighted. Why not? A man's mind – what there is of it – has always the advantage of being masculine – as the smallest birch tree is of a higher kind than the most soaring palm – and even his ignorance is of a sounder quality. Sir James might not have originated this estimate; but a kind Providence furnishes the limpest personality with a little gum or starch in the form of tradition.

These are characteristically shrewd words by a very great writer but it struck me at the time that, applied to Wiltshire and me, they were unfair and that Mrs Leavis had mistaken the anxiety she inspired for arrogance. With as much, if not more nervous energy than her husband (like a demented bumble bee is how John Wiltshire has since described the impression she made on him), and her insatiable appetite for reading, she probably, in coming back to teaching after a long break, expected more from us that we could ever give. I have however to consider that from my arrival at grammar school until my first supervision with Mrs Leavis, I had only ever been taught by men and, though I was not aware of it at the time, and certainly cannot identify it now, there may have been something in my attitude which betrayed what I felt to be the unfamiliarity of the situation.

One way of categorising Mrs Leavis's disapproval would be to call it my first brush with feminism. There was a painful moment in my adolescence when I was jeered at by a group of mill girls, headscarves tightly tied under their chins to keep the cotton from flying into their hair; but since I was wearing my grammar school blazer at the time, that incident may not have been gender related. One would have thought that awareness of the quiet unhappiness of several of the women I knew at home would have given me an insight into the injustices of their position. My mother, for example, having worked before her marriage for a Scottish carpet manufacturer in Manchester, had badly missed earning a wage and the conviviality of the workplace when she was restricted to those home duties for which she had no natural taste. When she became a 'dinner lady' at the local primary school it was less (I suspect) because of the pin money involved, although that must have come in useful, than to get out of the house. There were others in her position in my immediate environment, yet whatever understanding I drew from those cases was countered by the strong sense I had when growing up of living in a society that was matriarchal. The women who mattered to me may have been economically dependent but, as far as I was concerned, they were the ones with all the authority and who therefore lived richer, more satisfying lives than their husbands. Having abandoned responsibility in the domestic sphere, my own father lost all power within it. This dominance of the women I knew might have made me a conservative supporter of the status quo had there not been other aspects of the way relations between the sexes were then arranged which were more painfully direct. At grammar school we were better off than our contemporaries in the private sector in that there was an equivalent institution for girls just down the road. But the virtual apartheid which was in operation added immeasurably to the miseries of adolescence and is hardly justified by the thought that it provided good training for a university where there was one female student for every ten who were male.

Perhaps the biggest social change which has occurred during my lifetime, or rather the one of which I have been most conscious, is the gradual empowerment of women. I was made most aware of it through my daughters but also by the rising number of my female colleagues (although that would have to have risen much further to match the usual ratio of one male to nine females in the last English literature seminars I taught). This is an ongoing process, far less advanced in other spheres of social life, and its justice is so patent, and its benefits so obvious, that the occasional adverse side-effects it may have had on individuals like me cannot be significant. One of these became evident recently after I had written a short book about Byron. I have very little interest in Byron's so-called serious poetry, *Childe Harold* and the like, but have always been fascinated by the comic poems he wrote towards the end of his career, *Beppo*, *The Vision of Judgement*, and of course *Don Juan*. I also very much enjoy his letters. There is a tone in these which I tried to characterise by repeating a story Byron himself told in response to his publisher's complaint that there were in the manuscript of *Don Juan* he had been sent 'approximations to indelicacy'. The phrase reminded him, Byron replied, of an exchange he had had in Cambridge with George Lamb, the son of Lady Melbourne, who was a woman notorious in her youth for the number of her lovers. 'Sir', Lamb had protested to Byron in reference to Scrope Davies who was a friend of them both, he 'hinted at my illegitimacy'. Asked whether this was true Davies had apparently replied, 'Yes, I called him a damned adulterous bastard'. This evidently tickled Byron, as it does me, but I can see that it has something of the smoking room about it and that, more generally, his humour is redolent of a society in which men spend a lot of time with each other and develop a culture of 'joshing' (as I once heard a female colleague refer contemptuously to the way some men talk to each other). There are, I am sure, thousands of women who enjoy Byron's letters, and thousands more who relish his *Don Juan* (Germaine Greer being one), but I felt in some of the reviews of my book by female academics a certain distaste for the aspect of Byron I had chosen to foreground and that their remarks placed me on the wrong side of an unbridgeable gulf. In the relations between the sexes things have moved on so rapidly that some of us are left stranded with tastes and habits of mind that the predominantly male environments in which we grew up developed in us. I see no point in being apologetic about this, even if I can in my own case regret that I was slower on the uptake about certain matters than I might have been. There are however ways in which I feel sorry, and in a manner that reminds me of the words of a song made popular in the 1950s by Connie Francis, although it had been composed thirty years previously. I heard this song frequently when I was growing up without recognising its vibrant note of female anger, and it was only later that I felt fully the appositeness of its last verse (repeated and bawled out by Francis in a different key):

> Right to the end, just like a friend
> I tried to warn you somehow;
> You had your way, now you must pay
> I'm glad that you're sorry now.

If I had continued to associate freely with girls after leaving primary school, I might have been much quicker to appreciate their point of view. Appreciating the point of view of women is something the male reader learns from George Eliot (whom I read avidly), but that is hardly feminism, and if Mrs Leavis's use of Sir James Chetham against Wiltshire and me did represent a brush with that movement, the touch was of the lightest, most passing kind. She herself was after all hardly what would now be called a feminist. That is clear enough in a notoriously scathing review she wrote in the early days of *Scrutiny* of Virginia Woolf's *Three Guineas*, a book which she felt was even more of 'a let-down for [her] sex' than *A Room of One's Own* had been. *Three Guineas* strikes me now as a bold attempt to answer a difficult and significant question. How will it be possible, Woolf asks, for women to continue to infiltrate the male professions without at the same time acquiring the aggressive, competitive values associated with them? The progress of her argument is not always very direct, and her ironies are often too insistent, but her book has some excellent moments and certainly did not deserve the scandalously unfair and inaccurate account Mrs Leavis gave of it. Woolf's logical processes, she remarks at one point, are reminiscent of Dickens's Mrs Nickelby while their effect is of 'Nazi dialectic without Nazi conviction' (this was in 1938). So much animus, you feel, must in part be personal and one motive for it can be found in the book's extensive notes. Woolf uses these chiefly to document grotesque injustices of the recent past and particularly the way in which women from well-heeled families were deprived of higher education while every sacrifice was made to send their brothers to public school and Oxbridge. But in one note she elaborates on a view she has expressed in the text that lecturing on English literature in Cambridge is 'vain and vicious'. The violence with which one school of literature is opposed to another, she writes, can be attributed to 'the power which a mature mind lecturing immature minds has to infect them with strong, if passing, opinions, and to tinge those opinions with personal bias'. The allusion is almost certainly to the influence the Leavises were having, and even if it were not, Mrs Leavis appears to have taken it as such. Her response was vitriolic and she is remorseless in tracking down weaknesses in *Three Guineas*, as well as in discovering several it does not have. Although Woolf makes it clear enough that she is only concerned with a small group of women from the upper middle-class, Mrs Leavis lambasts her for having too little general experience of life to pronounce authoritatively on her topic and produces in the process the excellent joke for which her review is still best known. Quoting Woolf to the effect that 'Daughters of educated men have always done their thinking from hand to mouth ... They have thought while they stirred the pot, while they rocked the cradle', Mrs Leavis comments acidly: 'I agree with someone who complained that to judge from the acquaintance with the realities of life displayed in this book there is no reason to suppose Mrs Woolf would know which end of the cradle to stir'.

The Woolf review shows Mrs Leavis as someone who did not mind making enemies, a fact that only partially explains why, although she published a good deal and worked tirelessly with her husband to keep *Scrutiny* going (while at the same time bringing up three children), she was never offered a permanent university post. In *Three Guineas* Woolf reflects on the twenty years that the English civil service had been opened up to women and notes with some bitterness that the average annual salary of those who had managed to establish themselves there was still far below that of the men. Illustrating some of the prejudice which she feels accounts for the discrepancy; she defines what came to be known in later feminist parlance as the glass ceiling. If anyone ought to have been sympathetic to that notion it was Mrs Leavis. An important first move in establishing a successful academic career is to choose a good Ph.D. subject, find a publisher for the results, and then hope that they will be well received. *Fiction and the Reading Public* had been Queenie's research topic (she was supervised by I. A. Richards) and even one of its most hostile critics described its first appearance in print as causing 'something of a sensation'.

The subject of her book is how the reading public referred to in its title was radically transformed by the growth of both democracy and capitalism, and how forms of writing were developed which were designed to satisfy the newly emergent segments of its composition. Her approach was original – she must have been the first researcher in English to make use of questionnaires (sent to a number of popular novelists) – and remarkably wide-ranging. The amount of reading the book entailed was prodigious, especially in the undergrowth of second or third-rate novelists from her own and previous centuries. It manifested a combination of sharp intelligence with phenomenal industry and contained as well as implied a store of knowledge which would be very useful to Leavis – whose own reading tended to be intense rather than extensive – when he shifted his main focus from poetry to the novel. At Girton Queenie had been a star pupil, carrying off all the prizes, and Muriel Bradbrook, her contemporary there, would later describe in an obituary how unusually ambitious and dedicated she was. Leavis was one of her supervisors while she was an undergraduate and may have had some influence on her Ph.D. topic since he had himself recently completed a dissertation on the influence of journalism on literature which was similarly concerned with the evolution of the reading public, and also surveyed the field from Elizabethan times onwards. That remained unpublished (attached to it in the Cambridge University Library is a note from him advising students not to bother with any photocopying because the thesis was written 'before research became an industry'), whereas the appearance in print of her own work meant that she was later acknowledged as a pioneer in the new field of literary sociology. Most of her successors wrote from a Marxist point of view which was certainly not hers even if, in an early review in *Scrutiny*, she does refer scathingly to those individuals from the middle classes who in 1926 helped to break the General Strike.

Fiction and the Reading Public proved to be important and influential; without the efforts of Mrs Leavis behind the scenes *Scrutiny* would have collapsed; and her later work on Jane Austen, and many other novelists, came to be highly regarded. That she nevertheless never received any kind of official recognition for all she had done had begun to embitter her by the 1960s, although it never seems to have made her more of a feminist. That avenue was closed off by the essentially conservative narrative of cultural decline which she and her husband had elaborated and which included, in some of his own later writings at least, hints about the damage done to society by women taking over roles previously allocated to men. *Fiction and the Reading Public* was an essential building block in that narrative. In the course of it Mrs Leavis quotes twice a passage from Thomas Nashe (him again), using it as an illustration of the degree of mental agility Elizabethan readers must have possessed in order to follow what was at the time a very popular text, and then contrasting that with the mental lethargy which the rise of journalism and the development of the popular novel had fostered in their twentieth-century equivalents. Even in the eighteenth and nineteenth centuries, she argued, the conditions for self-improvement among the lower classes were favourable largely because there was not that multiplication of 'frivolous stimuli' which were to appear later. Nowadays, she went on,

> The temptation to accept the cheap and easy pleasures offered by the cinema, the circulating library, the magazine, the newspaper, the dance-hall, and the loud-speaker is too much for almost everyone. To refrain would be to exercise a severer self-discipline than even the strongest-minded are likely to practise, for only the unusually self-disciplined can fight against their environment and only the unusually self-aware can perceive the necessity of doing so.

By the time John Wiltshire and I were growing up there were no more circulating libraries and I suspect that in Derby where he lived, and where his father was a foreman in the Rolls Royce factory, he spent no more time in the dance-hall than I did in Swinton and Pendlebury. In *Fiction and the Reading Public* as a whole, however, there is a reasonably accurate sketch of both our cultural backgrounds before the appearance of even more 'frivolous stimuli' than the most direly pessimistic observer could have anticipated, so that it strikes me now that what may have disappointed Mrs Leavis in us was not only our supposed male chauvinism but also our failure to manifest enough of that unusual self-discipline and self-awareness to which she refers here. All too typical products of a degenerate culture is how she may have been inclined to see us.

SEVEN

CLASS

The person who described *Fiction and the Reading Public* as causing 'something of a sensation' was a Cambridge lecturer called F. L. Lucas. For him, the book was full of 'angry arrogance' and a symptom of the unfortunate emphasis on *criticism* in the teaching of English at Cambridge. 'The more I see, in education, of Criticism in its ordinary sense of judging books – what the elect call "evaluation"', he wrote, in a manifestation of fellow feeling with the Oxford don who had rebuked Robert Graves, 'the more I doubt its use'. He complained that what Mrs Leavis's denunciation of the popular culture of her day heralded was a new Puritanism and, classically trained himself, rather weakened his proposals for changes to the Cambridge English Tripos by confessing he could see nothing in it that could compare to Classics 'as education'. 'The study of its two literatures is saved from the effeminacy of many aesthetic pursuits by its linguistic difficulty', this former Rugby schoolboy elaborated, 'from muddle-headedness by the clarity of the classical mind, from critical crazes by its remoteness'. By the time he wrote these strange words Lucas was a fellow of King's and an intimate of Woolf and the Bloomsbury group. The hostility between these people and the Leavises was sociological as well as ideological, as much a matter (that is) of class as of differing views. As the remark about not knowing which end of the cradle to stir indicates, the review of *Three Guineas* is not so much an attack on Woolf as a feminist, but rather as an over-privileged woman insulated from the realities of the world by her class, and therefore incapable of commenting sensibly on them. It is written from the perspective of a double outsider, someone who not only came from a relatively modest social background but who was also Jewish. Queenie Roth was Mrs Leavis's name before she married. Because of his own last name, Leavis himself was also thought to be Jewish, especially by an unpleasant variety of his enemies. But if he had have been, Queenie's parents would have had no reason to cut her off completely when she married him. The quarrel was bitter and, although the claim has been disputed, she is reputed never to have seen her mother again.

Leavis was not as it happens Jewish but in some ways as much an outsider as his wife. That his father was the relatively prosperous owner of a piano shop in Cambridge, did not stop him being a local boy from the wrong side of the tracks. There was no disguising his origins because he spoke with a strong and much-imitated regional accent. It is hard now to realise the difference this must have made in his early days when the vast majority of Oxbridge dons would have sounded like Brian Sewell. In his dislike of Bloomsbury, just as in his wife's hostility to Virginia Woolf, there was therefore a good deal of class antagonism and I remember he used occasionally to refer disparagingly to those dons who had the good fortune to live in huge houses in the area of Cambridge around Grange Road.

Neither of the Leavises was at all posh and that created an atmosphere at Downing which suited me. I found it a congenial home in a university whose predominantly public school ethos filled me with a social discomfort I never entirely got rid of during my whole time there. I had had an anticipatory sign of how things would be when I was interviewed during the entrance examination process. My interviewer had nothing to do with English but was a church historian called Stevenson and I have often wondered since what role he was meant to play: whether, if my written work was satisfactory, he was empowered to intervene and say 'I don't think this is the kind of chap we want at the college' or, if it was below par, he could pull rank and insist that the cricket team needed a wicket-keeper. The conversation we had together was anodyne enough but at one moment – he must have had something like a headmaster's report in front of him – he said that he saw I played football. When I agreed that I did, his eyebrows went up to the accompaniment of a mildly enquiring 'First fifteen?' We both knew immediately we were at cross purposes and it may be that the minor embarrassment the mistake cost Stevenson helped my cause. When I later came to Downing, he was my 'moral tutor', and a pleasant enough man. I am sure that if I had fallen grievously sick, or into the hands of criminal money-lenders, he would have done his best to help. As it was, he discharged his responsibilities towards me largely through the annual administration of a sherry of gut-wrenching asperity and dryness. There was in the Cambridge of the 1960s some mysterious equivalence between sherry and social refinement: the drier the one, the greater the other. It was as if a rumour had reached its purveyors that blowsy, working-class women in Northern pubs pig out on the sweet variety when they tire of their port and lemon. Stevenson's sherry was of the type which when spilled on the hand makes the skin pucker, and in having to drink it, I felt like a Cherokee brave at an initiation ceremony. But perhaps I only put it this way because the drink I describe was served at what was oxymoronically called an annual 'sherry *party*', and I am loading on to its innocent, alcoholic head the awkwardness which the occasion generated in me. It must have been fairly early in my time at Cambridge that I read Evelyn Waugh's *Brideshead Revisited*. The first part of that book, with its description of the narrator's meeting in Oxford with Sebastian Flyte and his teddy bear Aloysius, summed up many of the things I most disliked in Cambridge. How I felt about them was crystallised for me much later when I went to dinner with a colleague in Kent whose wife was from a working-class family in Wales and had trained as a primary school teacher. She described how she had been for a long time on 'supply' (temporarily filling gaps when other teachers were off sick or not immediately available), and had been sent at one point to a school in a particularly bad state of repair. She remembered opening the door on a classroom where posters were half-hanging off the wall, there was broken furniture, and a number of ragged children running about, many of them from gypsy families. Once she was inside, one of the little boys picked up a book that was lying on the floor, looked accusingly at her, and said, 'Not Winnie the fucking Pooh again'. Whenever I think of Sebastian Flyte and Aloysius, this little boy comes into my mind.

'Fucking' is not a word I use easily, but it strikes me as appropriate here. In 'A propos of *Lady Chatterley's Lover*', a text I would much rather re-read than the novel to which it refers, Lawrence writes of having wanted to rehabilitate words of this kind because they form 'a natural part of the mind's consciousness of the body'. If common sense had not told me that this was a hopeless task, memory of the months I had spent on a building site would have. 'Fucking' seems somehow right when it is juxtaposed with Pooh bear because of the surprise and incongruity, but I am not so sure about its use in another anecdote that happens to have stuck in my mind. I first heard this in a radio programme about Frank Randall, a music-hall figure from my father's generation. All these Lancashire comics interested me although my particular favourite was Jimmie James, one of whose quips has always helped me to characterise the sub-culture of semi-continuous comic banter which surrounded me as I was growing up. James worked with stooges (like Falstaff with Bardolph), and the most memorable of these was a tall, thin and gormless individual called Eli. But it is another, sharper stooge who comes to James at one point and says to him aggressively, ''Ere, have you been putting it around I'm stupid'. 'Why', James replies, puffing neurotically on a cigarette in what was always part of his comic business, 'Did you want to keep it a secret?'

Randall was for me a much less funny comedian than James and, although he made several films, he seems to have had less success beyond his native ground. But there he was revered and a regular in Blackpool, that Mecca of all Lancashire comedians. The anecdote I heard concerned a time when he was asked to attend a civic reception given by the Mayor of Blackpool. His agent took him there with some trepidation, knowing how unpredictable his client could be on formal occasions. He was relieved therefore when the initial presentations appeared to be passing without incident: 'How nice to see you, Mr Randall', 'I'm very glad to be here' and so on. But then just as Randall was turning away, the Mayor somewhat pompously solicited his attention again and, pointing to the woman at his side, said, 'The Lady Mayoress, my wife'. 'Well', replied Randall, 'that's your fucking fault, isn't it?'

There is a comic effect here which, as in the case of Winnie the Pooh, depends heavily on the expletive. The reason it makes me slightly uneasy is not, I'm afraid, because it is cruel (so much of comedy is), but because it causes me to think about my own attitudes to authority and privilege, or at least those which, like the gypsy boy, I may have inherited. I had almost no contacts of what might be called an aesthetic nature with my father. What I can remember best was playing his small collection of 78 records endlessly, especially those which featured comic songs and, more especially still, the one which had Leslie Sarony singing 'Ain't it grand to be blooming well dead'. The only words of this well known item which I remember as being in any way witty were: 'Some folks there were praying for my soul / I said it's the first time I've been off the dole'; but the situation of a man watching all the fuss surrounding his own funeral makes it grimly humorous throughout. I never spoke to my father about this song so that the only actual conversation we ever had about the art available to us both involved a film, or rather an episode from a film which had clearly made a lasting impression on him but which I myself had never seen. As he told it, a humble clerk played by Charles Laughton learns that he has won a million dollars and makes his way to the head office where he gives his managing director an aggressive and patently valedictory V sign. I seem to remember my father chuckling at the way this was represented and adding to his account a V sign of his own as an indication of how much the memory of the episode continued to please him. Very much later the name of Charles Laughton, Yorkshire born but priceless in *Hobson's Choice*, allowed me to trace this episode to a short segment which Ernst Lubitsch had contributed to one of those portmanteau films popular in the 1930s called *If I had a million*. Laughton's performance is striking, sufficiently so to be on YouTube, but what is curious and distinctive is that, after learning of his windfall and making his way up the stairs of the building where he works, past office after office of assistant directors and secretaries, the bank clerk he plays pauses in front of a mirror to adjust his tie, and when he enters the director's room does not give him the V sign – the film is American and the V sign is not after all the potent gesture in the States it once was in Britain – but blows him instead what is both a childish and contemptuous raspberry. I imagine that my father, wrapped up in the significance of the moment as he must have been, had adapted the episode for his own emotional purposes.

What kind of dissatisfactions and frustrations my father might have suffered in his working life is unknown to me, and nor do I know if they were at all connected with the devastating clinical depression which descended on him once he had retired. In recalling the Laughton episode, he may just have been participating in that traditional hostility to those above us in the social hierarchy which Frank Randall and the gypsy boy were expressing in their very different ways. But the fact that I have retained memories of both forces me to wonder what my state of mind was when I first went up to Cambridge and whether there were oblique ways in which I could have been accused of being a snob. In my sense of that word, the one I grew up with, a snob is a person who uses largely adventitious advantages, such as wealth, accent, social status or even good looks, in order to look down scornfully on others. When I began to read Jane Austen, I found striking instances of what I understood by it in *Pride and Prejudice*'s Lady Catherine de Bourgh or, even more spectacularly, in *Persuasion*'s Sir Walter Elliot. That there could be any other kind of snob hardly crossed my mind until I read in Cyril Connolly's *Enemies of Promise* a discussion of the low status accorded to their masters by the boys at Eton. A majority of these boys, he writes, assumed that 'most of the staff had never held a gun or worn a tailcoat, that they were *racked by snobbery*, by the desire to be asked to stay with important parents or to be condescended to by popular boys'.

It must, I imagine, be snobbery in this sense, of wanting to be better than you are and mix with those higher up in the social scale, to which Eliot is referring when he accuses Lawrence of 'a certain snobbery' in *After Strange Gods*. The charge comes after he has claimed that Lawrence creates characters 'without any moral or social sense'; that he is incapable of 'what is ordinarily called thinking'; and that he had a 'deplorable religious up-bringing'. Eliot never republished *After Strange Gods* – there were remarks in it about Jews which came to seem increasingly unpleasant after it had first appeared in 1934; but Leavis refused to allow him to forget what he had once said. He deals with the snobbery charge in the second chapter of *D. H. Lawrence: Novelist* where his chief weapon is 'Fanny and Annie', one of a group of excellent short stories which had a special interest for me because they deal with characters who have broken away from their home environment but then return to it, either temporarily or, as in Fanny's case, for good. She has been a ladies' maid and hoped for better things than her background might have led her to anticipate; but at the age of thirty she has come back to her grimy provincial birthplace and a foundry worker called Harry whom she has for several years kept dangling. In a splendidly comic scene, Lawrence describes how she discovers that Harry might well have fathered an illegitimate child while she has been away. After digesting this news, she decides to marry him after all and embrace that working-class woman's lot she had previously been keen to escape. In considering Lawrence's handling of these events, Leavis writes, it never occurs to us to suggest that 'snobbery is a word called for by any element in the situation'.

Although what Leavis says strikes me as irrefutable, it is a puzzle why he should have chosen 'Fanny and Annie' to challenge Eliot on the question of snobbery in the first place since there seems very little room in this short story for a display of snobbish attitudes. It is true that Fanny is described as having had social aspirations, but we never see her outside a working class environment, and there is therefore no possibility of her revealing the snobbish features of that desire to become part of a higher social world which, according to Connolly, the Eton boys detected in their masters. If the Oxford English Dictionary is anything to go by, his definition of snobbery is the dominant one (it is within its parameters that Virginia Woolf was clearly working when she gave that talk to her memoir club called 'Am I a snob?'); but there are situations in which it meets and combines with my own. In *Persuasion,* Sir Walter Elliot is indignant when he learns that his daughter Ann will not be accompanying him on a visit he intends to make because she is engaged to see an old school friend who adds to the injury of living in the unfashionable Westgate Buildings, the insult of being called Smith: what is Miss Ann Elliot doing consorting with such people? This is classic snobbery in my own initial understanding of the term. Yet the reason he is quite so indignant is that the visit Ann says she will have to miss is to Lady Dalrymple, whose rank is higher than his and who has previously scarcely acknowledged his existence. The true, complete snob (that is) looks both down and up. There are no opportunities in 'Fanny and Annie' for the heroine to look up because everyone in the story is more or less on her level; but it could be thought she looks down when Lawrence is describing, from her point of view, what it is about the man she has decided to marry which distresses her. One of Harry's strengths is a fine tenor voice which he has been prevented from making the most of by his pronunciation. 'His solos were spoilt to local fame', Lawrence writes, because when he sang he handled his aitches so hopelessly.

> 'And I saw 'eaven hopened
> And be'old a white 'orse'

This was one of Harry's classics, only surpassed by his heaving:

> 'Hangels – hever bright an' fair'

It was a pity, but it was unalterable. He had a good voice, and he sang with a certain lacerating fire, but his pronunciation made it all funny. And *nothing* could alter him.

In George Eliot and Hardy, and even in Dickens, this kind of light comic effect is almost always accompanied by condescension (that close cousin of snobbery). Extracted in this fashion, the words here may sound condescending but it seems to me that, in context, the falsity of that impression becomes very clear and that, knowing the world he is dealing with so intimately, Lawrence never takes away from Harry his own integrity (it is a strength as well as weakness that nothing could alter him), nor represents Fanny as a snob who looks down anymore than she looks up.

Whether or not 'Fanny and Annie' represents the best ground on which to refute Eliot's charge against Lawrence, refuted it surely is by Leavis. And yet in defending Lawrence from another accusation, closely associated with snobbery, it strikes me that he goes too far. It is virtually impossible to talk about snobbery in England without also talking about class so that Eliot not only accuses Lawrence of 'a certain snobbery' but also claims that 'no writer is more conscious of class distinctions'. 'No writer', Leavis responds, 'is more wholly without class-feeling in the ordinary sense of the term'. This is wrong as anyone who takes the trouble to trawl through Lawrence's letters, and especially those written towards the end of his life, can quickly discover. In the ordinary or any other meaning of the word, Lawrence had a great deal of class feeling and I suspect this was also true of me when I first arrived in Cambridge. I am reasonably certain that I was not a snob in the sense that I aspired to be like the public school types I met and copy their clothing or speech, as one Yorkshire boy did who came up with me and in no time at all was wearing a bow-tie and bereft of his broad regional accent. But it took me a good while to make friends with those who spoke quite differently from the way I did and whose clearly superior education I did not have to envy; and if I continued to remember what Frank Randall said to the Lord Mayor, it may be because I found some relief for my own class feelings in the very direct expression of his.

EIGHT

POLITICS

As Lucas's review of *Fiction and the Reading Public* might suggest, King's College, with its strong Bloomsbury connections, was often a centre of opposition to the Leavises. It was to another of its fellows, 'Dadie' Rylands, a former Etonian who, like Lucas, had begun his academic career in Classics and then switched to English, that Maurice Bowra wrote in order to give his impression of Leavis at about the time I was being taught by him. This was also the period when Leavis was developing a small following in Oxford so that it is almost certainly there that Bowra would have seen and heard him.

> He had nothing to say, but the whole mystery was revealed. He is what our mothers would have called CHAPEL. The low, mousey voice, trailing into inaudibility at the end of each sentence, so suitable for the ministrations of the Lord's supper; the quotations from scripture in the form of Lawrence and James; the moral themes, *Little Dorrit* above all *good*, Dickens stands for life (eternal no doubt), to deny it is *sin* ... above all the sense that if you sign with him on the dotted line, you are saved ... I can now understand why our miserable undergraduates brought up in Little Bethels and Mount Zions and Bethesdas feel at home with him as with nobody else, especially as his Salvation means a great deal less work than the ordinary methods of studying the subject.

There are thirty years between Lucas's review of Mrs Leavis and what Bowra says here, but some of the complaints remained constant: that the Leavisian approach was in the Puritan, non-conformist tradition, for example (Lucas had talked of Ben Jonson's Zeal-of-the-land Busy), or that by putting literary criticism at the heart of his conception of English, Leavis was offering his students an easy ride. But what is striking is the snobbery of Bowra, in his reference to what 'our mothers' used to say but more especially in his talk of those 'miserable undergraduates' who in the early 1960s Oxford had become obliged to accept. They were presumably the ones for whom Leavis was having some appeal and Bowra's contempt for their cultural background is very similar to that of T. S. Eliot for the 'Chapel' upbringing of D. H. Lawrence. The Chapel Lawrence knew, Leavis had responded tartly, 'was the centre of a strong social life, and the focus of a still persistent cultural tradition'. The intellectual education of those young people that it nurtured in the 1890s 'was intimately bound up with a social training, which, even if it didn't give them Wykehamist or Etonian or even Harvard manners, I see no reason for supposing inferior to that enjoyed by Mr Eliot.'

Since there was often a strong degree of class feeling between Leavis and his enemies, the question I used to ask myself later was why that had not eventuated, on his part, in some form of left-wing politics. Certainly when I went up to Downing there was no sign of such a thing. In saying that I am using hindsight since my own background did nothing to help me notice its absence. I would if challenged have called myself a Labour supporter and could never have thought of voting for the Tories; but my interest in, and understanding of politics was shamefully small. When I read in Terry Eagleton's brilliantly witty memoir that in Cambridge he found time to act as a volunteer for Meals on Wheels, in addition to his more obvious political commitments, I have to wonder again what I did with my spare time at university. In an attempt to expiate some of the guilt they felt at finding themselves in such a privileged situation, some of my Downing contemporaries tried to fraternise with the college porters, as the nearest representatives of the working class on offer. But I never warmed to them. Punctilious enforcers of petty regulations – those were the days when you could still find yourselves locked out if you came back to the college too late – they seemed to me like bad-tempered NCOs for whom the little authority they enjoyed acted as a drug, and I particularly hated the degree of scorn and sarcasm they were able to inject into their obligatory 'Sir'. When this word was addressed to me, I always felt that they were registering how disappointed they were by the quality of students now coming up to Cambridge and regretting the days of the gilded youths in boaters who would call them 'my good man' and slip them half a guinea.

It is of course possible to become a Trotskyite, or join the Socialist Workers' Party, in middle age; but youth's the more usual time to begin these affiliations. It is I suppose some sort of explanation that as I was growing up

I was not aware of being myself the victim of any major social injustice, nor conscious of anyone in my immediate environment who had suffered one (no doubt I did not look hard enough). But my failure to become a political radical may have had less to do with specific incentives than my general lack of what in the eighteenth century was called enthusiasm. In class terms, I certainly qualified as one of the 'miserable undergraduates' Bowra refers to, but there was no Little Bethel or Mount Zion in my background and a distinct lack in my whole family group of any tendency to be swept away or taken up. At its weakest, this was just apathy or indifference; at its strongest, a healthy vein of scepticism inhibiting any commitment which risked becoming too intense. I can illustrate this latter version in relation to my great Aunt Peggy. She was my rich aunt (everyone should have one), the youngest sister-in-law of my maternal grandfather who had married into a family of many girls. Of the other ones we used to visit I remember well Aunt Ellen who was so old that the trek to see her would later remind me of the villagers going to consult the wise old man who lives alone, outside the village, in *The Seven Samurai*. She was poor in comparison with my grandmother and particularly with another of the sisters, my aunt Min, who had married a bluff Manchester business man called Bert Parker. They had been able to retire to Eastbourne where I visited them during one summer holiday. Uncle Bert had too much energy to be retired. His son Ross by a previous marriage had written the music for Vera Lynn's 'We'll meet again' and he himself was musical, although he only played by ear. Every day at five to twelve in Eastbourne he would sit at the piano and nervously strum a tune or two in order to indicate, business man as he always was, that he needed his lunch on time. Very kind to me, Uncle Bert was the person who, when I was very young, may be said to have stimulated my interest in poetry by giving me half-a-crown to stand on a coffee table and recite 'Albert and the Lion'.

> At this the manager had to be sent for
> He came and said, 'What's to do?'
> Ma said: 'Yon lion's eaten our Albert',
> Pa said: 'And 'im in his Sunday clothes too'.

Even today this is the only long poem I have no difficulty in recalling in full. Perhaps it was the money.

The great aunts were one of my first introductions to human variety and the greatest of them all was undoubtedly Aunt Peggy. She lived in a splendid detached house in East Sheen called 'The Sanctuary'. Her husband had held some well-paid position in one of the private rail companies and been required to travel a lot (I remember that my mother took it as a sign of his importance that he had had his teeth fixed in Poland); but at some point he had retired to devote himself to Spiritualism. I imagine that it was for faith healing rather than communication with the dead that he became well-known since it was this first power which was transferred to his wife on his relatively early death. Aunt Peggy 'laid on hands' and successfully enough to fund – whether through direct fees or bequests – what to us in Swinton and Pendlebury seemed an opulent life-style. I was sent to stay with her in 'The Sanctuary' once and can recall sleeping in a box room surrounded by pile upon pile of old copies of *The Psychic News*. There was another little room close by, with a red light outside. When that light was on, I was given to understand, I needed to be careful not to disturb Aunt Peggy because it meant she was in the room and communicating with her guide in the spirit world. At the time it struck me as very odd that this guide was a Native American, but I learned later that they were common intermediaries in Spiritualist circles.

I saw my Aunt Peggy on several subsequent occasions and she was among the very few of my relatives who came to my wedding in Paris where members of my wife's family were delighted by her pink hat ('just like the Queen'). But our relationship did not flourish chiefly, I suspect, because I never showed any interest in her work and may even have betrayed the complete disdain for it so often expressed at home. The most I ever heard from my mother or her sister was grudging admiration for the extent to which Aunt Peggy had bamboozled the world. We were a sceptical crowd and that I took my scepticism up to Cambridge meant that, in comparison with one or two of my fellow students, I was only ever a tepid Leavisite. In some ways, however, that was appropriate in that there were occasions when Leavis himself had offered a model of scepticism and had clearly not found it easy to commit to a cause. His career had begun in that atmosphere of profound cultural pessimism, generated before the First World War but then massively increased by it. His diagnosis of what was wrong was in several respects close to that of the Marxists, although it owed more to the Christian socialism of R. H. Tawney. The trouble had started in the sixteenth and seventeenth centuries, Leavis believed, with the breakup of the old rural communities by a rapidly expanding commerce. This had begun the long process whereby man's work lost contact with the rhythm of the seasons and the labouring masses were shifted into towns to become slaves of the machine. One result may have been more leisure but that was hardly an advantage for the alienated worker when meaning had gone out of his life and he had been left a prey to all those forces which Capital develops to distract its victims from the sterility of their existence. When *Scrutiny* was launched in the early 1930s there was an on-going crisis in Western Capitalism felt by many to be terminal. In its third number Leavis wrote an article in which he said that he did not see why 'supporters of *Scrutiny* should not favour some kind of communism as the solution of the economic problem'. Yet at the same time, he strongly opposed committing the journal to any particular political line and criticised even Trotsky, in his view much the most intelligent of the leading Marxist thinkers on cultural affairs, for the crudity of his ideas about relations between a nation's economic life and its literature.

Leavis refused to commit himself to a political cause in the 1930s and, despite the flurry of excitement in the 1960s when he announced in the papers that he would be voting Liberal (he withdrew his support from the local Liberal candidate after he had spoken of the 'standard of living' solely in economic terms), never showed any serious signs of really doing so later. Several avowed Marxists wrote for *Scrutiny* in the early days but there was no likelihood of his characterising himself in that way. Aspects of his analysis of what was wrong with the world may have resembled theirs, but there were crucial differences of emphasis. He recognised just as much as they did the dependence of literature on its social context but was anxious to highlight intellectual or spiritual determinants as well as those which were economic. They tended to compare the contemporary situation with what it might one day become whereas he was always inclined to look back to what it had once been. The reason he gave a qualified approval to Trotsky was that he had dismissed the notion that, after the Revolution, culture would begin anew and recognised instead that it would be a question of the Proletariat appropriating and transforming the best elements in the bourgeois culture which had gone before. Trotsky acknowledged, that is, the need for some *continuity*, a key term in Leavis's vocabulary. That in his view a major function of the literary intellectual was the rescue and preservation of what was best in the literary and cultural past meant that there was always a conservatism built into his account of what Capitalism had destroyed.

This tendency in Leavis's thinking comes out best in his enthusiasm for two books by George Sturt, *Change in the Village* and, more particularly, *The Wheelwright's Shop*. I remember that we always used to mention this last title with self-defensive jocularity as if we were instinctively aware that it led to what was not the strongest aspect of our teacher's thinking. Sturt describes in *The Wheelwright's Shop* how, in the 1880s, he took over from his father a business in a remote Surrey village where carts, and especially the wheels for carts, were being made virtually without machinery, and according to a craftsmanship that had been handed down from generation to generation and had been in operation for hundreds of years. The tone of his description can be judged by his account of seeing in later life one of the carts of the kind he had once made piled high, not with the hay for which it had been intended but with bricks (for the building of villas that would 'desecrate some ancient heath or woodland or field'):

> Instead of quiet beautiful cart-horses, a little puffing steam-engine was hurrying this captive along, faster than ever farm-wagon was designed to go. The shafts had been removed – as when Samson was mutilated to serve the ends of his masters – and although I couldn't see it, I knew only too well how the timbers would be trembling and the axles fretting at the speed of this unwonted toil. I felt as if pain was being inflicted; as if some quiet old cottager had been captured by savages and was being driven to work on the public road.

The Wheelwright's Shop is in many respects a finely written book but I was a poor audience for it. A complete urbanite, I had failed to distinguish myself in my school's woodwork classes which were taken by a man called Jones who doubled as a gym teacher and was notorious for blaring in a Welsh accent at those who had forgotten their shorts, 'You'll do gym naked, boy!' Having been bowled over by the section in Pascal's *Pensées* called 'Misère de l'homme', I was receptive to Leavis's account of the general poor state of contemporary society and of where popular culture then stood ('Distracted from distraction by distraction'); but I was not so sure it had ever been much better. Sturt's employees may well have had far more satisfaction in their work than Chaplin's frantic factory hand in *Modern* Times, or those I had met on the assembly line in Kellogg's, but quite how much more they would have had to have had in order to compensate for their long hours, poor pay and scant provision for sickness and old age was not clear to me. Besides, even the exquisite craftsmanship involved in making a good cart wheel might become tedious, and therefore unsatisfying, when you have been doing it over and over again for thirty years. A further satisfaction the employees enjoyed, Sturt implied, was integration into a traditional social organisation where people cared for each other and there was a general acceptance of mutual duties and responsibilities, where, in the words of Tawney, society was 'a spiritual organism, and not an economic machine'. This is what Leavis used to call the 'organic community'. That gave to its members both the security and comfort of knowing where they stood but chiefly because, it seemed to me, there was never ever much likelihood of their being able to stand anywhere else.

A major feature of my training at Downing was its emphasis on particularity. We were taught always to be specific, to try as often as possible to give examples, and never to use vague, abstract words. Leavis often made it clear that the past by which he measured the shortcomings of the present could never be recovered, elliptically enforcing the point on one occasion by saying he had not the slightest interest in Morris dancing; but as far as I was concerned, the difficulty in his thinking on this topic was that it was so general. I came across an example of what I mean in a late essay of his on Eliot's 'Burnt Norton'. At the beginning of the poem, Eliot depicts the English peasantry of the Tudor period as somewhat oafish ('Rustically solemn or in rustic laughter / Lifting heavy feet in clumsy shoes, / Earth feet, loam feet ...'). Yet these were the same people, Leavis protests, 'who created the English language – robust, supple, humanly sensitive and illimitably responsive and receptive – and made possible in due course Shakespeare, Dickens and the poet of *Four Quartets*. A language is a cultural life, a living creative continuity'. Trying to come to terms with this claim (don't we inherit language more than we create it?), I pointed out to a friend that if, as all the scholars say, the English language was in a particularly vibrant and expanding state when Shakespeare came on the scene, it was as much because of the economic and cultural forces which broke up the village communities Eliot is describing as of those communities themselves. But he merely nodded wearily and cited Popper's remark that, when you see someone struggling in a bog, the last thing you should do is jump in after him; and it is true that there is not much to be made of the very broad cultural generalisations about the past which both the Leavises were inclined to make throughout their careers. Perhaps they were right to believe that the disappearance of the organic community has brought us immeasurable loss; but if so 'immeasurable' becomes an appropriate word and there is then a great deal of difficulty in defining the 'us' referred to in the formulation. Any statement about the cultural well-being of a past society or community considered as a bloc is vulnerable to the citing of exceptions. This is why, in spite of F. L. Lucas's glaring prejudice and unfairness, a remark he makes about Mrs Leavis's notion of entertainment for the masses being on a steady downward curve remains relevant to what she and her husband had to say on that subject long after *Fiction and the Reading Public* had appeared. 'It is surely a great deal better', he wrote, 'to like the trashiest fiction than to enjoy seeing a witch burnt, or to go to the silliest cinema than to soak in an eighteenth-century gin-shop'.

The details of Leavis's take on the past left me sceptical but I fully accepted his Manichean view of the present and the evidence from the newspapers or radio he periodically adduced in support of it. Yet since these were indicative of a deeper malaise associated not just with literary culture but culture as a whole (the way people live their lives), how could there be any effective means to transform the situation outside of politics? It would be fair to say that Leavis's only proposed solution was guerrilla warfare. We students were to be an elite brigade sent into the world to support good work and expose false standards wherever we found either. The fact that our activity would be in the literary realm, in the use of words, did not make it peripheral given that view of the English language as 'a cultural life, a living creative continuity' he espoused. Language was central to living – politics after all had largely to be conducted in it – so that literary criticism was not like some nineteenth-century accomplishment but rather a discipline that mattered to society as a whole. Had not Leavis in any case declared, in the very first number of *Scrutiny*, that it was 'the best possible training for intelligence – for free, unspecialised general intelligence' and was it not the case therefore that our striving to become competent literary critics was simultaneously an effort to contribute to all aspects of social life? That at least was the idea and it was a sufficiently intimidating challenge to make most of us at Downing feel that any involvement in ordinary politics could only be a distraction from the real tasks ahead.

NINE

FRANCE

Although it was soon suggested to me that the word referred to the three-legged stools on which students formally sat their examinations, I thought it was typical of Cambridge that the English *Tripos* should be divided into only two parts. In my first weeks there, I was asked to go for a supervision on Chaucer with a supervisor who lived in an outlying village called Coton. Having been to the bookshop and bought a second-hand Chaucer which turned out on inspection to be a nineteenth-century translation, I jumped on my bike and made off in the general direction of where I thought the village might be. If I had asked my way in the part of Lancashire I came from, I would have been showered with too much help. On this occasion the natives were surly and uncommunicative when I enquired of several of them where Cotton was. If any of them twigged that I was pronouncing the word wrongly, they were not going to let on. The single 't' in the real name of the village does perhaps suggest 'coat' but, although the confusion may on that occasion have been my fault, I take no blame for the bafflement I felt initially when several people I met referred to a college called 'Keys'. It took me some time to realise that this was Gonville and Caius. These linguistic traps were everywhere in Cambridge and once they were mastered, you yourself could stand by and watch the uninitiated fall into them. I suppose Caius/Keys could be celebrated as a quirk of history which has left its mark on the language (like the use of Tripos), but it comes about because the founder of the college, who was plain John Keys, wanted to latinise his name. I discovered a more extreme case of a similar phenomenon when I read a biography of the Earl of Southampton – the man to whom Shakespeare dedicated his two long poems – and found that the family name had originally been Writh before an ancestor who died in 1504 decided that it would look more aristocratic spelt Wriothesley.

The examination for Part One of the English Tripos came after two years and it was as I was working towards it that I must have begun to feel uneasy about what I should do once I had left the university. In those days, as I think perhaps still in these, you could lengthen out your degree to four years by interrupting your studies at home and spending a year abroad. A number of foreign governments, including the French, would pay you enough to live on while you taught a little English in one of their schools. The scheme was designed chiefly for students of foreign languages but I had heard that it was also open to people like me and therefore applied. I had made only one short visit to France by this time, but even that had turned me into a Francophile. If I needed to find a non-literary reason for this, I would have to focus on something as trivial as lettuce. This only ever appeared in my home as decoration, although the Welsh teachers who lived next door to us in Pendlebury, and who were in their way refined, used sometimes to serve crisp pieces of lettuce at tea-time, sprinkled with sugar. It was on that first short visit to France that I came across the habit of serving salad after the main dish and felt that any culture which had invented vinaigrette had to have a lot going for it.

The school I was sent to was in Evreux, in Normandy, and was what the French used to call an *école normale*. Evreux had been much damaged in the war and was not, I felt, a particularly attractive or welcoming town. The school had found me a room in a hotel which was attached to a night-club. During the week, I seemed to be the only resident and the night club was virtually silent; but at the weekends there was a great deal of noise and a constant sound of footsteps up and down the hotel's corridors. I soon found I was living in what was virtually a brothel and this came about because, in those days, France was still a member of NATO. There was an American base just outside the town and my hotel cum night-club was the one favoured by the black soldiers. There was an equivalent set-up close by where all the white soldiers went. Relations between the two groups were poor and fights often broke out. The advantage of my hotel was that the music from its night-club was sophisticated. The rival establishment lived on a diet of country and western which I regret now I hardly ever heard. I understand that in country and western music you often hear the same tune, and that the harmonies are utterly predictable; but I have always liked the resigned pessimism as well as the humour of many of the lyrics, and the plangency of the female singers.

At the appointed hour, I reported for duty at the school and was introduced to the headmaster. He was a short, dapper individual in rimless spectacles and a well-cut suit, every inch the efficient bureaucrat. At the time

I could read French quite well but was incapable of saying very much. There was in any case a delay in my grasping what was said to me so that I was not in a position to respond appropriately as I began to glimpse what the headmaster was explaining. The English teacher was still on maternity leave, it appeared, and he would like me to fill in for her. My understanding had been that a language assistant was required to talk English to small groups and not teach a class in the ordinary meaning of that term; but the headmaster was calling on me to help him out in an emergency. I may not have been able to speak much French but was I not, after all, someone who was studying English at Cambridge University (like all my relatives and my father in paticular – 'Don't you already speak it?' – he took 'studying English' as a reference to the language)? Before I could formulate some method of escape, he led me down several corridors, opened the door on a classroom full of restive male adolescents and, after a few introductory words, left me to my own devices. Afterwards, I thought he had been like the zoo-keeper who opens the lions' cage, throws in some raw meat and calmly walks away.

When people hear the words *école normale*, they usually think of the *école normale supérieure* in Paris where Sartre and many other of those who dominated the French literary scene after the Second World War received their university education. My *école normale* was a very different kettle of fish. It was part of a country-wide network of what in English might have been called teacher training colleges. If they were bright enough, children from working and lower-middle class families went to them from the age of about 16, in order to complete three years of higher education at no extra cost to their parents. They were fed and boarded, even perhaps paid a small allowance, the hitch being that they then owed ten or so years of their professional life to the French Ministry of Education. The boys that faced me in that classroom, therefore, were far from stupid, not inclined to respect authority, and all in their mid-teens (girls were taught in another building). It was a total mismatch. In the general chaos, the only detail I recall is asking what their hobbies were and how many of them followed cycling. 'He does', one or two of them shouted, pointing to a boy in the second row and repeating several times the word *pédale*. Only much later did I recognise this as a slang term for pederast or, more generally, a homosexual. At some point I gave up the unequal struggle and went to sit behind the desk whereupon the tumult quietened down. There must have been other sessions that followed this one but not I think very many. Either because the English teacher returned, or the headmaster decided he had given me something I could not handle, my responsibilities were soon limited to chatting amiably with small, manageable collections of students and I was left to contemplate my second major failure as a teacher.

At certain moments in my life I have been the beneficiary of unsolicited and unmerited acts of kindness, which I was too selfish or self-absorbed to appreciate fully at the time and which it is now too late for me to reciprocate. One of the debts I owe and can never now repay is to Michel Maillard, the school's teacher of French Literature who was a graduate of the *école normale superieure* and made his reluctant way down to us from Paris two or three days in every week. France was then an even more highly centralised intellectual community than it is now. The universities and schools of its northern regions were full of teachers who refused to give up their base in Paris, for general cultural reasons no doubt, but also because preferment (moving from one post to another) was by ministerial appointment and Paris was where all the power lay. I was told later that Germany was not much better and people would jokingly claim that those unfortunate enough to have been posted to a provincial university always slept with the window open in case they missed the call (*der Ruf*) from the centre. Maillard discussed French literature with me and even corrected the grammatical mistakes in some observations, meant to be in the style of La Rochefoucauld, which I had written. He was a gentle, highly cultivated man and the first person I had ever met who wore glasses which darkened in the sunlight – he had particularly weak eyes. I suspect that those reflections in which I practised my French appealed to him because of their disillusioned tone. His view of life in Normandy was similar to that of its native son Flaubert, and he shared this writer's pervading melancholy and hatred of *la platitude bourgeoise*. If I couldn't quite match his enthusiasm for Flaubert, it may have been because he had become something of a whipping boy for Leavis who frequently contrasted Flaubert's concern for form and *le mot juste* with the energy and whole-heartedness of his nineteenth-century English contemporaries. I thought *Madame Bovary* a great novel but could not see any way round the complaint of an admiring Henry James that there was eventually a disabling mismatch between Emma's consciousness ('too small an affair') and her creator's own. This seemed to me true also of Frédéric Moreau, the hero of *L'Education sentimentale,* a novel which I was later made to feel, by friends who were Flaubertians, constituted the acid test of literary intelligence. Frédéric and his cronies struck me as tedious in their relative stupidity and selfishness, especially before the welcome diversion of an excellent description of the 1848 revolution; but when I voiced that feeling, I was told I had missed the irony. I didn't feel I had and that Flaubert's habit of looking down on his characters from a height was part of the problem. Whether I had been coached into this attitude – James's criticism of Flaubert was often mentioned in Downing – or that coaching in other areas had produced it, I find it impossible to say. It may be that this is what I would have felt in any case. 'But who shall parcel out / His intellect, by geometric rules, / Split, like a province, into round and square?', Wordsworth asks. 'Who knows the individual hour in which / His habits were first sown, even as a seed, / Who that shall point, as with a wand, and say, / "This portion of the river of my mind / Came from yon fountain"?'

After Christmas I was able to visit Maillard in Paris because I had moved there myself. He lived in Charenton, way out of the city, and in a flat miserable enough to explain his gloomy wife's fits of depression. It seems to me in retrospect that he might have been better off enjoying material comfort in the provinces than comparative squalor in the Capital, but that may be because I have since been corrupted by enviable scenes of provincial life in the films of Chabrol and others. At the time, I must have shared to some extent his sense of Paris as an island in a cultural desert and been able to move there because my duties at the *école normale* had become so minimal. I find it hard to account for what I then did with my time: wasted most of it, I imagine. As far as I remember, I had no particular plan and no particular focus. It would be ten or even twenty more years before I began to live according to what, when you are now proposing a new course at the university, are called 'aims and objectives' (hard to tell the difference). Sometimes I am inclined to wonder how much better I might have done in my professional life had I learnt to concentrate earlier, an especially crass not to say conceited form of counter-factual thinking. More often, in these days, I think how relaxing it would be to get up every morning with no agenda for the day and I remember that one reason Lawrence admired his wife so much was that she could spend hours lolling in a hammock with a cigarette in one hand and a book in the other. Frieda was an expert in happily wasting her time, something that, with his temperament and background, Lawrence had to try and train himself to do.

A good deal of desultory reading I must nevertheless have got through in Paris, chiefly in French, and I believe it was at this time that I scoured the *quais* along the Seine for an appropriate picture of Molière to hang on my wall. It pleases me to remember this as a rare indication of the 'enthusiasm' I was otherwise inclined to lack. The French reading was not irrelevant to my studies because in both parts of the Cambridge English Tripos there was a 'language paper': an opportunity to write about a foreign literature. Already in Part One I had studied various French classics, including Madame de la Fayette's *La Princesse de Clèves*. This is a favourite text for introducing students to French literature because it is so relatively short and the vocabulary is so limited. I was very taken with its psychological acuteness and its elegant concision. Nowadays it strikes me as a trifle thin but at that time the more pointed and economical a paragraph was, the more it pleased me. I loved the joke about the two men discussing what they thought was the best couplet in French drama. When one of them cites two famous lines from *Phèdre* – '*Ce n'est plus une ardeur dans mes veines cachée / Mais Vénus tout entière à sa proie attachée*', perhaps – the other responds that yes, they were quite good lines, '*mais il y a des longueurs*'. This taste I then cultivated was not the best preparation for a life as a teacher of English at the university. Of all the gifts the fairies could be asked to bestow on a child destined for that trade, the most useful might be what the rhetoricians call *amplificatio*. I have known colleagues who could spin a whole hour's lecture out of the most basic and obvious of propositions, and make it interesting. At one extreme this indicates no more than the inclination to waffle but at the other it becomes the ability, most evident in a writer like Dickens, to conjure wonderfully creative elaborations out of one simple fact or thought. Naturally short-winded, my inclination was always to look for briefer and more laconic ways of conveying what I had to say. If that sometimes saved me from being boring, it ignored how often the situation requires healthy flesh and not bare bones.

Being interested in French while studying English was not an anomaly in Downing because Leavis both read and spoke the language very well. He had after all spent four years in France. I can still quote from memory the beginning of Valéry's *Le Cimetière marin* ('*Ce toit tranquil ...*' etc.), because he intoned it to us so often. Modern French poetry had clearly been a strong interest for him and he was confident enough in his feeling for it to identify two moments in *Four Quartets* where he thought Eliot was echoing lines from Mallarmé. To believe you have enough French to be inward with such a difficult writer takes some doing: my own inclination was to leave modern French poetry alone. But Leavis was in general a good linguist. When I got back to Cambridge, he held seminars on the texts we were required to study for the Tragedy paper. For most students, the Tragedy course began with Aeschylus whom Leavis could read in the original. My own efforts with the *Orestia* for my supervisor consisted largely in taking one scene, noting how wildly different it was in three of the current translations, and deciding there was nothing that could be said. Much later, when I was teaching in Australia, I took the opposite view on the issue of translation from the one I developed then. The professor was a mild Leavisite and strongly opposed a scheme some of us concocted to introduce a course on the novel which included Tolstoy and Dostoevsky. My argument was the pragmatic one that however much of a distortion of Tolstoy's work even a good translation of *Anna Karenina* might be, it was still obviously worth study (and hadn't Leavis himself written an essay on the novel?). His was that the most characteristic procedure of the teaching of English as Leavis had first conceived it, the examination of linguistic texture – the 'words on the page' – became impossible when those words were clearly not Tolstoy's own.

The Tragedy course centred around Shakespeare, but it also included Racine. It was because of Racine that I have my only clear memory of standing up to Leavis. This will seem pusillanimous (only *one* memory), but I was a reasonable creature and the arguments he could deploy against a writer I had enjoyed, or in favour of one who had left me cold, usually gave me pause. They appealed to that notion of the better self which Matthew Arnold invokes when he describes how we can, for example, read a text with qualities which we instinctively feel are there but cannot quite grasp. My standing up to Leavis came about because he had asked me to say a few words in the seminar about *Phèdre*. I can still see the expression of amused scepticism with which he met my eager exposition of Racine's virtues. In the discussion that followed there were no doubt references to the straightjacket of rhyming couplets (in comparison with Elizabethan blank verse); thoughts on 'the language of Shakespeare' (an expression which in Leavis tended to carry echoes of cultural patriotism); and perhaps allusions to Dr Johnson's demolition of the case for the three unities in his *Preface to Shakespeare*. On all these issues I had nothing much to say in favour of the French, but I still stuck doggedly to my feeling that *Phèdre* was a remarkably moving and powerful play, even if I thereby aligned myself not only with Bloomsbury but also with Clifford Chatterley, who enjoys reading out Racine's plays to Connie. When around this time I was working on Wordsworth, I was struck by the passage in the Preface to *Lyrical Ballads* where he is explaining why he has not changed several expressions which some of his readers have regarded as faulty. 'It is dangerous to make these alterations on the simple authority of a few individuals, or even of certain classes of men', he writes,

> for where the understanding of an Author is not convinced, or his feelings altered, this cannot be done without great injury to himself; for his own feelings are his stay and support; and, if he set them aside in one instance, he may be induced to repeat this act till his mind shall lose all confidence in itself, and become utterly debilitated.

There is an element of comedy here in that Wordsworth was never one to pay very much attention to what other people said: you don't lead a revolution in taste without having immense self-confidence. In the history of science there are several instances of thinkers who have clung on to a particular theory despite what seemed at the time effective demonstrations of its falsity, and have proved in the end to be justified. Wordsworth was like one of those thinkers. Of course, the same history has also left traces of thousands who have refused to accept perfectly sound refutation of their crackpot ideas. In continuing to admire Racine I knew I was not a crackpot and I was dimly aware of the psychological importance of safe-guarding from Leavis at least one area where I knew what I really liked. Later, in my own teaching, my ambition often reduced itself, not to imposing my taste on the students but asking them to work out what they *really* liked. Since many of those who say they know what they like are misinformed, this is a task which, for both student and teacher, is not as simple as it sounds.

TEN

THE RICHMOND LECTURE

I arrived back in Cambridge to find that Leavis had become what might now be called a celebrity. In my first two years, I had often been made aware that there were circles in which he was well known. Asked by certain people where I was studying English, I had only to tell them Downing to see a wary glint appear in their eyes. But these were a minority in the know whereas now everyone I met seemed familiar with his name. The reason was the text of one of his lectures which had appeared in *The Spectator* and been followed by an avalanche of mainly hostile correspondence. As his students, it was not only indirectly that we were implicated. In one letter to *The Spectator*, for example, there was an explicit reference to us as 'a band of analphabetics who, young and foolish, applaud his cold contempt for writers he does not understand' while, in another, the world was told that we did not need to read extensively because 'Dr. Leavis knows which are the good books worth reading'. When one correspondent wrote that Leavis could have been cheerfully left alone in his 'lower middle-class Bethel' were he not someone who exerted a great deal of influence, we also felt ourselves targeted.

The cause of all this fuss was a lecture which had been given in Downing in February 1962, while I was still in France. It was part of a series established in honour of a naval historian who had been a previous master of the college, Admiral Sir Herbert William Richmond, and Leavis may have been invited to give this particular one because he was about to retire. He later claimed that it was largely a college affair and that he only passed a full text on to *The Spectator* because misleading accounts of the occasion had been leaked to other parts of the press. His subject was 'The Two Cultures', the title of another lecture which had been given more than two years previously by C. P. Snow, a fellow of Downing's near neighbour Christ's and someone who, after being involved in important scientific research, had gone on to become a prominent government advisor, but also a best-selling novelist. Snow's starting-point was the wholly justifiable claim that in England there has always been a prejudice in favour of the humanities and against applied science. Deploring the ignorance science and arts graduates display of each other's subjects, he called for wholesale reform of the educational system which would bring the two closer together and then, in a rather big leap, went on to say that the West would need to produce far more technocrats if the growing gap between the world's rich and poor was ever to be closed (and for him, that gap was as great a danger to mankind's future as the hydrogen bomb or over-population). These are large topics and there are repeated signs in the lecture that Snow's ratiocinative powers had taken on much more than they could comfortably handle; but there were also certain, more apparently superficial aspects which particularly irritated Leavis. One was Snow's assumption that he straddled the two cultures and had the authority to talk about both of them because he was a scientist and a writer. In Leavis's view, the quality of Snow's novels did not entitle him to the latter title. Another was the clear proof of Snow not being a writer in frequent infelicities of style, especially when he attempted to strike a more popular note. Regretting, for example, that most of the major nineteenth- and twentieth-century authors had not understood the industrial revolution, he exempted Ibsen and then added the unfortunate 'and there wasn't much that old man didn't understand'. Commenting on the rapidity with which the Russians and Chinese were able to industrialise their economies, he wrote that they had proved how 'common men can show extraordinary fortitude in chasing jam tomorrow. Jam today and men aren't at their most exciting, jam tomorrow, and one often sees them at their noblest'. For Leavis, the style was so often the man that anyone who expressed himself in this way was not simply a poor writer but incapable of serious thought.

At the heart of Leavis's objection to Snow was precisely this question of industrialisation. Accusing most literary intellectuals of being 'natural Luddites', Snow had declared that 'industrialisation is the only hope for the poor' and, citing his own family background as evidence, claimed that 'in any country where they have had the chance, the poor have walked off the land into the factories as fast as the factories could take them'. Talk of this kind was a direct challenge to Leavis's belief that the industrial revolution had been a disaster for the *quality* of English social life, and he criticised Snow for contemplating the salvation of the Third World's poor through technology without considering what would be lost in the process. Rising out of a sea of surrounding abuse of Leavis, the author of an editorial in *The Spectator* bravely made the essential point when he criticised 'the cult of science and technology without an adequate sense of moral purpose' and then added 'it is the business of writers, philosophers and moralists [Leavis presumably falling into this third category] to represent those values which alone can give life to culture or direction to the vast human achievement of science'.

Leavis's lecture would not have excited so much controversy had he made his points in the same way as the author of *The Spectator*'s editorial, but in its opening especially he was nothing if not polemical. Characterising Snow's tone as one which only genius could justify but which it was hard to imagine genius adopting, he claimed that, far from being a genius, Snow was 'portentously ignorant' and 'as intellectually undistinguished as it is possible to be'. His lecture on the two cultures was not only 'a document for the study of cliché' but exhibited 'an utter lack of intellectual distinction and an embarrassing vulgarity of style'. 'Frightening in his capacity of representative phenomenon', Snow was for Leavis 'utterly without a glimmer of what creative literature is, or why it matters', and his lecture was hard to discuss because, when you looked for a mind to argue with, there was no mind there. Phrases such as these inevitably produced a reaction. In *The Spectator* correspondence there were references to 'the reptilian venom of those who have created nothing' and to Leavis as 'the Himmler of literature'. Of the seventeen letters which *The Spectator* published in their first number after the lecture had appeared (many more would follow), only two had anything to say in his favour. The low point was reached early in a very long opening letter by William Gerhardi (an old enemy). Commenting on the way Leavis had appealed to D. H. Lawrence in support of his argument, he wrote: 'The doctor's infatuation with his shaggy god is like the "pash" of an hysterical schoolgirl viciously jabbing her pencil into the back of any girl daring to utter one word of criticism of her adored mistress'.

The virulence of the attacks had the inevitable effect of banding Leavis's students closer together and making them feel more important. His criticism of the slack thinking of a major Establishment figure, someone who (in a phrase Snow himself had coined) frequented 'the corridors of power', more firmly defined our own identity as outsiders. A student who had been in my year before I went to France managed to have a short letter of his own included in a second batch *The Spectator* published (there would be a third). Describing the initial attacks on Leavis as a 'first-rate document for the condition of our time', he quoted words of Ortega y Gasset about 'the progressive triumph of the pseudo-intellectual, unqualified, unqualifiable and, by their very mental texture, disqualified' before ending: 'Sir, I suggest that it is Dr. Leavis who is the truly qualified man'. The reference to Ortega y Gasset was not surprising. This student had amazed us all when we first arrived in Downing by the breadth of his reading and his encyclopaedic knowledge. He also had a photographic memory and could recite lines of poetry at will. When I told him that if I tried to quote a poem from memory, I usually got a few words wrong, he replied that in that case he did not see how I could have read and appreciated it properly, an objection I then found, and still do find, hard to counter. He had graduated by the time I returned to Cambridge but a lively group which had been in the first year when the Richmond lecture was given profited now from the cool reception accorded the recent republication of *Scrutiny* by Cambridge University Press, and sprang to Leavis's defence with a pamphlet entitled *The Ogre of Downing Castle*. Its centrepiece was a well-sustained exercise in irony by Howard Jacobson describing how Leavis had surrounded himself with wicked men, 'though none so wicked as himself', in order to launch a 'vile and pernicious magazine' and 'sow corruption, rot, and unwholesome tendencies in the Nation's youth'.

Although I took no active part in these rearguard actions, my sympathies were wholly with them and, as far as the outside world was concerned, I was a fully paid-up member of the Leavis group. Privately I had some doubts, all of which were to do with me rather than him. My scepticism about my own worthiness was general but, when I look back, it now seems as if it principally revolved around two points. The first was that I was far from being an assiduous reader of poetry. I had enjoyed the Metaphysicals and much of the rest of the poets of the seventeenth century, found Pope and the other eighteenth-century poets very interesting (even developing a taste for Jane Austen's favourite, Cowper), and been captivated by Wordsworth. But after that my enthusiasm waned and it largely disappeared as I approached the twentieth century. Early Eliot I enjoyed but I struggled with the middle and late work, mainly because I felt there was a lot of it I could not fully understand. If I had known then what I know now about his debt to the French symbolists, I might have tried to mount a case against poetry which deliberately sets out to be obscure. My trouble was that Eliot was a key figure for Leavis. When he first encountered his work during and after the First World War, he had clearly felt that here at last was someone capable of dealing with modern concerns in an appropriately modern way. Later on he would decide that the poetic strength of the English language had migrated during the nineteenth century into the novel and, in the Richmond lecture, offer *Women in Love* as an example of a work in which the confusions of the early twentieth century were diagnosed 'both discursively and by the poetic means of a great novelist'. Yet previously it had been Eliot who was the writer in the right kind of touch with his time and enough of his admiration remained for us to feel it was the task of the critic to recognise and respond to the challenges set by such an original poet while at the same time being on the lookout for the next writer who would similarly demonstrate the continuing vitality of English by stretching its boundaries. Dazzling as I found many lines in Eliot's later poetry, it gave me much more pain than pleasure and I certainly did not feel qualified to discriminate among the younger poets who continued to write in a Modernist vein.

This was only a minor failure or betrayal, but there was lurking a much greater and more fundamental one which I would never have been able to articulate fully at the time. In his attack on the soulless materialism which he felt Snow displayed in his discussion of how the lot of the Third World's poor might be relieved, Leavis quotes a favourite phrase of his from the first chapter of *The Rainbow* ('How Tom Brangwen Married a Polish Lady'). This occurs after Tom has caught sight of Lydia Lensky for the first time and immediately decided she should be his wife. He then begins to worry he might not be accepted but 'during the long February nights, with the ewes in labour', Lawrence writes, 'looking out from the shelter into the flashing stars, he knew he did not belong to himself'. It was this last phrase about belonging which became talismanic for Leavis although the passage then goes on: 'He must admit that he was only fragmentary, something incomplete and subject. There were the stars in the dark heaven travelling, the whole host passing by on some eternal voyage. So he sat small and submissive to the greater ordering'. Glossing this passage in *D. H. Lawrence: Novelist*, Leavis noted with implicit approval that it had often been said of George Eliot, 'by way of a limiting judgement', that she was 'ethical' rather than 'religious' and added that Lawrence, by contrast, was quite clearly a religious writer. Equally clear was that this non-doctrinal kind of religion, which Lawrence manifests in so many different ways and on so many occasions, was something Leavis himself shared and that it was a lack of any *spiritual* dimension in Snow which he so deplored.

In those early days I was fortunately only dimly aware that I did not have much of a spiritual dimension either. When Lawrence is speaking auto-biographically, and describing the feeling of not belonging to himself, the context is invariably his relation to the natural world. But I was a city boy or, more accurately, a suburbanite. I could not walk out of my front door and be, as he could, into the countryside in a few minutes. My only experience of 'Nature' was on very occasional family outings and then my attitude was only mildly appreciative, rather like those country-lovers of the late eighteenth century, before the Wordsworthian revolution. The implications of this escaped me at the time, and yet I ought to have had some inkling of where I stood after an incident at my grammar school. Before the arrival of Derek Beard, we had for a short period an English master who seemed to us bizarre in that, after morning assembly, he would be seen still kneeling down, and could occasionally be glimpsed praying at other times of the day. At some point when we were discussing the countryside, or Nature in general, I began arguing that it was much less important than the Romantic poets suggested and that Dr Johnson was right to say that anyone who was tired of London was tired of life. It seems strange to me now that I should have maintained this point of view when I have come to hate London, and all big towns, but I suppose I was showing off. The English master looked at me incredulously and, after a considerable pause, said, 'Then you can have no religious feeling'. In the sense in which Leavis defines the word religious, he was probably right. The only comfort I could have taken was that to be 'ethical' with George Eliot was always going to be a reasonable second-best.

Downing English allowed for a great deal of diversity, but on these two fronts of modern poetry and religion, I was obscurely aware of falling short. Not that it mattered much as I trundled on through my last year and towards Finals, sweating to extrude one crabbed sentence after another for my supervisors, and finding in a reference by Pope to those who can only squeeze eight lines a year from 'hard-bound brains', the perfect description for my constipated state. Painful as this could be, at least it meant that I was (at this time) in no danger of earning Leavis's displeasure for the cheap journalistic fluency which was for him a major scourge of contemporary cultural life, and which he found amply illustrated by Snow. His critics responded by repeating the familiar charge that he himself did not know how to write. One correspondent in *The Spectator* went so far as to call him 'scarcely literate' while another said how revealing it was that 'a notoriously bad stylist should attack Snow for a lack of style'. Leavis certainly did not write with the ease of Lord David Cecil whose style was once recommended to me at school on the grounds that he was able to dispense with commas. The reader is always made to feel behind his own writing the hard struggle to define the matter in hand with as much precision as possible, and the resulting sentence structures are often challenging. And yet he was responsible for countless formulations which became memorable because they seemed so felicitous, as well as considerable variety of tone. If he is often difficult to read, it is usually because he is presenting a subtle argument. Whatever else one might want to say about it, the Richmond Lecture is powerfully argued; although it is true that it would not have had the effect it did if it had not also been a rhetorical *tour de force*.

His delivery of this lecture may well have been a turning point since it seems to me that in most of the writing Leavis did afterwards he became increasingly mannered and over-dependent on a number of key terms he had invented. 'Technoligico-Benthamite' is a prime example. This was his way of characterising what was wrong with modern civilisation, reliant on the successors to the early twentieth-century machine, and incorrigibly utilitarian in spirit; but in my view he fell back on it too often and in a way that suggested he was no longer thinking hard about the mass of complex phenomena it represented; or contemplating what might have been gained as well as lost by 'progress'. It became for him a buzz word and his dependence on it, as well as on other expressions of the same kind, was accompanied by a developing weakness for foreign expressions, very surprising in someone who was always praising the abundant richness of the English language. In his late analysis of Eliot's *Four Quartets*, for example, he decides that he can not properly convey his meaning without the help of two German words, *Ahnung* and *Nisus*; and he frequently refers, for no legitimate reason I can see, to Eliot's *procédés*. By this stage, the prose in that analysis has become tortured enough to highlight the paradox that, although in his later career Leavis's commitment to Lawrence strengthened, the way he wrote increasingly approximated to Henry James in his last phase. This in spite of his section on that novelist in *The Great Tradition* being full of neat descriptions of quite what he feels is so unsatisfactory in late James. 'The developed and done is exasperatingly disproportionate to the laboured doing', he states at one point, and at another he asks: 'Isn't the energy of the "doing" (and the energy demanded for the reading) disproportionate to the issues – to any issues that are concretely held and presented?' In some of Leavis's later writings, and especially those which deal with social issues, there is similarly more manner than matter, as well as a tendency to browbeat rather than persuade the reader. So lean and spare in his early days, the elaborate circumlocutions of his late years seem much less frequently forced on him by the complexity of the matters in hand as indulged in for their own sake.

ELEVEN

LOOSE END

Because the end of Finals left me at a loose end and I found nothing better to do, I wandered back to France. There must have been in either London or Paris an office which dealt with the distribution of French assistantships since I remember going there in the summer and asking whether there were any of what at that late point would be 'returns' or cancellations. Given the circumstances, I ought to have found myself trying to teach English to small groups somewhere in the Morvan, or a run-down area of one of the industrial cities, but instead I was offered a post at the *lycée Charlemagne* in Paris, a result no doubt of a late withdrawal and my having arrived in the office just at the right time. This school competed for status with prestigious *lycées* such as *Louis-le-Grand* or *Henri IV*, but it was located in the 4th arrondissement, which at that time was in a dilapidated condition, more in tune than now with its being traditionally known as *le Marais*. It was full of fine old buildings, including those of the early seventeenth century in the *place des Vosges*, but in the 1960s most of these were suffering from what vintners would have called *pourriture noble*. Not long after I had stopped working there, it began to become fashionable again and was extensively as well as expensively renovated. A sign of its position today is that when the retiring head of the IMF, Dominique Strauss-Kahn, was finally allowed to leave America and arrived back in Paris, the journalists tracked him back from the airport, not to Neuilly or the 16th, but a luxurious flat in the *place des Vosges*.

When I had lived in Paris eighteen months before, I had rented a room from a retired couple out in the northern suburbs. This time I applied for a place in the *Collège Franco-Britannique*, one of many halls of residence for foreign students in a complex of buildings in the 14th arrondissement known as the *Cité internationale universitaire*. Founded after the First World War as a further manifestation of the *entente cordiale*, the *Collège Franco-Britannique* was when I lived there in the charge of a university professor of English called Robert Ellrodt. With expressionless eyes, a largely shaven head and hollow cheeks, he reminded me of an austere prelate in a portrait by Titian and I found his public persona deeply unsympathetic. Privately I attributed the gaunt, exhausted look to his having recently completed a *doctorat d'Etat* (it was on the metaphysical poets and had been published in three volumes a couple of years before). This was the supreme qualification in the French university world and the gateway to its high posts of command. The word was that it never took less than ten years to complete and that its chief characteristic had to be a staggering accumulation of scholarly information. In turning over the pages, the examiners needed to be made aware of thousands of days spent in the library reading books that had hardly ever been read before (or would be again), and of a search for other commentators on the subject which had left no stone unturned. Apart from the fact that they make scant or perhaps even no mention of Leavis or *Revaluation*, this was certainly a feature of Ellrodt's three volumes.

The spirit of the *doctorat d'Etat* was antithetical to everything I had been taught at Downing, as was the university world in which it was regarded as a crowning achievement. French universities were in one sense much more egalitarian than the English in that the only qualification for being able to go to them was to pass the baccalaureate. But the result was more students than the system could cope with, and hardly any possibility in the humanities of effective seminar work, let alone a supervision. The main teaching method was the *cours magistral*, where hundreds of students listened to a professor telling them what they could usually just as easily have found in books. To become such a professor you needed qualifications but also, since the posts were few, the right kind of influence and support. Once in post the rewards were very great and when I was in Paris there were tales of professors of English who spent four days a week in the capital, travelling on the fifth to some provincial university in order to give a couple of lectures before quickly returning and leaving lowly local subordinates to mark essays and generally pick up the pieces.

It does not say much for my character, or the effect of my Downing training, that having the impression of French university life I did, I began to nourish an ambition to become part of it. With a very poor sense of how protectionist the system was, and how many regulations existed to make it difficult for foreigners to teach the literature of their own language in France, I at least understood that I would have somehow to acquire a French qualification and made enquiries about enrolling for a doctorate, not the State version that I fantasised had reduced Ellrodt to a member of the living dead, but the far less valuable *doctorat d'université*, which was supposed to be completed in two years. I can remember going to see a couple of high-profile academics from the Sorbonne with a proposal involving French translations of Shakespeare, one of them a specialist in comparative literature, who seemed very full of himself, and the other a gentle, subtle-minded literary critic who was suffering from the onset of Parkinson's disease. The vagueness of their welcome corresponded to the vagueness with which I had formulated my topic, and the thoughts about how I would support myself while I was doing research.

If I nevertheless remained keen to somehow become a part of French intellectual life in spite of the (for me) rebarbative example of Ellrodt and others, it was partly because I was also in contact with much more encouraging models. At the *lycée Charlemagne*, for example, I had become friendly with an extraordinary young language teacher called Erik Veaux. The son of a country doctor, the 'k' in his first name gave the hint that his mother was Swedish and that he had therefore been brought up as a bi-lingual. It was not however her language that he taught at Charlemagne – there would have been no call for it – but Russian and perhaps Polish (a couple of years before, he had been a student in Warsaw and, getting to know the avant-garde theatre director Jerzy Grotowski, had translated some of his work into French). Erik introduced me to a small group of concentration camp survivors who were living in Paris, some of them on pensions provided by the German government. Prominent among them was Piotr Rawicz who had been initially rounded up as a Ukrainian and had somehow survived Auschwitz, perhaps by concealing his Jewish identity. He had recently published a successful, prize-winning novel about the holocaust (later translated into English as *Blood from the Sky*), and used to amuse us by describing how, when he first came to Paris as a correspondent for communist newspapers in the Soviet bloc, he would sit in a café drinking coffee and invent stories about how the seething proletariat was just on the point of open revolt in far away towns such as Clermont Ferrand or Marseilles.

The talk in this group was chiefly about literature, in many different European languages, and Erik himself certainly had a strong literary bent. But his interests were very wide and he had a remarkably quick grasp of complex matters together with a wit which, in a reflection of my reading at the time, I thought of as typically Stendhalian. As a language teacher in a *lycée*, even a highly prestigious one, he felt he was punching below his weight and talked of trying to make a late entry into one of Paris's *grandes écoles*. The three most important of these give their graduates advantages similar to the ones enjoyed by those who have been to Harvard or Yale in the United States, or to Oxford and Cambridge in England. In addition to the *École normale supérieure*, for students interested in philosophy and literature, there was the *École polytechnique* for physicists and mathematicians; but then also the *École nationale d'administration* (*l'Ena*), the breeding ground for diplomats and an embarrassing large number of members of any French government of recent times (there will always be more *énarques* close to power in Paris than even the number of Etonians in the present British cabinet). All three of these institutions had been founded during Napoleonic times as a way of countering the influence of wealth and family background and making, as Napoleon himself put it, *la carrière ouverte aux talents*. Over the years the rich have found ways of giving their offspring a better chance of getting into these schools than their less well off or well-born competitors; but a sign of Napoleon's ideal of a meritocracy not being completely dead in the 1960s was that one way of securing a place at *l'Ena* was to sit a competitive examination open only to members of the French public service. As a teacher, Erik was regarded as a public servant and it was for this examination or *concours* that he decided to prepare. Eventually he was successful and I later heard that he had become a commercial attaché in some French embassy. That saddened me a little because I remembered him as so irreverent and anti-Establishment; but only recently I noticed that, in what was presumably his retirement from the diplomatic service, he had become well-known in Paris as a translator of Polish prose and poetry.

Erik was a joy to be with and I spent more time with him, and other of my colleagues at the *lycée*, than I did with my compatriots at the *Collège Franco-Britannique*, most of whom were registered for graduate degrees back home and were busy researching away in Paris libraries. The one close friend I had in the *Cité universitaire* was a denizen of the so-called Swiss house (*la maison Suisse*). Jean-Marc Berthoud's origins were in Lausanne but he spoke perfect English because his father had been a missionary in South Africa, with a parish as big as Wales. One effect of knowing him was that I first became aware of the Leavisian diaspora. Jean-Marc had read English and History at a South African university and encountered there several teachers who were *Scrutiny* devotees. What had clearly impressed him was not only Leavis's insistence on the moral seriousness of any great work of art but also his belief that close attention to details of language could have a social and therefore political significance (a necessary faith for any fervent young intellectual choosing to spend his time reading English novels, plays and poems under the *apartheid* regime). Bringing from his missionary background a remarkable intensity and zeal, Jean-Marc would discuss various classics of English literature with me and refer in the process to passages from Leavis's writings which I had never read (or heard). The first person to make me aware just how widely Leavis's influence had spread, he was by no means the last to give me the uncomfortable feeling that being at Downing was a privilege I did not sufficiently appreciate. I saw a lot of him and was later to meet his siblings and widowed mother in Lausanne, although not his older brother who had earlier moved to England where he became a highly successful head of the English department in the University of York.

It was probably from Jean-Marc that I first heard about Henri Fluchère. Born near Manosque in the south of France, Fluchère had been the go-to man on French literary affairs in the very earliest days of *Scrutiny*. In the opening paragraph of a piece entitled 'The French Novel Today', published in June 1933, he had written 'My friend, Mr. F. R. Leavis, once remarked to me' so that it may in part be friendship which explains the appearance in December 1934 of an essay of his which deals with 'The Novels of Jean Giono', and which strikes a note of warm, undiscriminating enthusiasm not often heard in *Scrutiny*. On the other hand, the way Fluchère describes in this essay how Giono (who was also from Manosque) celebrates the lives of the shepherds and peasants of the wild Basses Alpes region, not so studded in the 1930s with second homes as it is today, may have had a special appeal for Mrs Leavis who was always on the lookout for evidence that there was nothing at all either morally or spiritually primitive about pre-industrial cultures. In 1946 Fluchère had left his home region to found and then run the *maison française* in Oxford; but he had very recently returned to a chair in Aix-en-Provence and I had the bizarre idea that, if Leavis could give me an introduction to him, I might go there to do my research. I did not then know Aix so that in retrospect this plan makes me think of that moment in *The Rainbow* when Ursula has decided she would like to find a position as a teacher away from home. One of the posts she sees advertised is in Gillingham and Gillingham, Lawrence writes, mimicking Ursula's day-dream, 'was such a lovely name, and Kent was the garden of England. So that, in Gillingham, an old, old village by the hop-fields, where the sun shone softly, she came out of school in the afternoon into the shadow of the plane-trees by the gate, and turned down the sleepy road towards the cottage where the corn-flowers poked their blue heads through the old wooden fence ...' The passage goes on in a way which is bitterly ironic for anyone who happens to live any where near Gillingham, as I do now. The contrast between dream and reality would not have been so stark in the case of Aix but what Lawrence is dramatising are preposterously unrealistic youthful thoughts, and I certainly had plenty of those.

Apart from perhaps enquiring what I should read while I was waiting to go to Downing, I had never made any kind of direct approach to Leavis so that it now seems to me very surprising that I should have asked him whether he could recommend or introduce me to Fluchère. He did send me the requisite letter but with what I remember as a certain veiled reluctance. This could have been because he disapproved of the strange and uncomfortable convention of letters of introduction. Another reason may have been that he did not think much of me, although certain phrases in his accompanying note suggested that it was rather that he no longer thought much of Fluchère. His track record on early friendships was not after all very good. A striking example was L. C. Knights who had been a close colleague and an editor of *Scrutiny* throughout the early years. He was someone Leavis used to talk about with disdain in our seminars, reporting that Knights had once said to him 'I am no moral hero', and always implying that he had dwindled into conventionality. In a letter to the *TLS* in 1972 he would accuse him of having 'an anti-*Scrutiny* attitude' and claim that, 'after the early years', his connection with the journal was 'not only negligible but deprecatory'. When on Leavis's death Knights wrote a personal memoir, he did not try to deal with the breach between them directly. Instead he pointed out that one of Leavis's own emphases in launching *Scrutiny* had been on co-operation, criticism in its 'essentially co-operative function'. Mulling over why from that point of view it had not been a complete success, he quoted Conor Cruise O'Brien's suggestion that 'the impairment of friendship by the demands of intelligence' might be a greater evil than 'the impairment of the expression of intelligence by the demands of friendship'; and also Burke's defence of being economical with the truth on the grounds that 'a man speaks truth with measure that he may speak it longer'. Although he does not say so, it is clear that he believes friendly co-operation with Leavis became impossible because (like Molière's misanthrope) he would have no truck with either of these positions.

The quotations from O'Brien and Burke have an application which is general but during the course of his memoir, and in the same context, Knights quotes a sentence from another former editor of *Scrutiny*, D. W. Harding, which seems nearer the bone. 'To leave his associates genuinely free to disagree with him without discomfort', Harding had written, 'is not characteristic of the self-assertive person'. These words come from an article by Harding which appeared in *Scrutiny* in December 1940 and was called 'The Custom of War and the Notion of Peace'. It argued for a model of human interaction different from the usual interplay between dominance and submission, with its possible outcome in violence and therefore warfare, for after all 'domination ... always involves a belittling of other peoples' social significance; they become helpers, or dependents, or employees, instead of companions'. The article was extracted from a book which appeared shortly afterwards and was entitled *The Impulse to Dominate*. Leavis used sometimes to refer to this work and wryly admit to us that he thought the portraits in it of dominant, self-assertive personalities were partly based on him. But this did not mean that he spoke of Harding in the same disparaging tone he adopted in referring to Knights. On the contrary, we were made aware of a respect consonant with several open avowals of intellectual indebtedness in his writing, and especially in the area of what, to echo the title of one of Harding's books, might be called experience into words. He used often to quote, for example, Harding's description of Isaac Rosenberg as a poet who 'brought language to bear on an incipient thought at an earlier stage of its development', and he was clearly both stimulated and challenged by what Harding had had to say in *Scrutiny* about Eliot's *Four Quartets*. Here was an early pupil and friend whose mind he admired, although he would sometimes mutter than anyone who went over to psychology was lost to literary studies – Harding had become a professor of psychology in London – and he was sceptical about the alternative models of social interaction proposed in *The Impulse to Dominate*. No-one who felt the need to make a difference in the world, he used to suggest, could do so without a certain amount of self-assertion and aggression. This is a view Harding himself would come close to endorsing in a memoir of Leavis significantly entitled 'No compromise'. He describes there how uncomfortable a colleague the young Leavis was for those Cambridge dons who regarded literature as 'one of the elegancies, a liturgical contribution to the sonorities of the combination room'; and how 'he refused to modify his personal response to a literary work – his insights and appraisals – by any deference to the standard evaluations'. The inevitable result was a great deal of hostility, and some persecution. Yet Leavis was essentially right, Harding goes on, 'in the conviction that standards of excellence were under continuous threat from the entrenchments of mediocrity', and he concludes by saying that he is left 'half wishing that [Leavis] had been different enough not to have had to endure, and to cause, so much unhappiness; but half convinced that a different person could not have done the particular work he had to do in face of rampant cultural inflation and the debasement of literary currency by influential people and institutions'.

When Harding talks of the unhappiness Leavis caused, he appears to be thinking chiefly of quarrels with old friends. Whether Fluchère was in fact an old friend with whom Leavis had quarrelled was something I never had the opportunity to discover since my plans for going to Aix-en-Provence soon evaporated as completely as do those of Ursula with regard to Gillingham. At some point during this year I must have asked one or other of my supervisors back in Cambridge whether there was any point in applying for a Government scholarship in order to do research in England. The reply

I received was encouraging and accompanied by an assurance that Leavis would lend his support. Given that all I had to offer was an upper second, the success of the application which I then made, and which settled my immediate future, may well have had a great deal to do with him. There was a paradox here in that the Leavises were always complaining, and with some obvious justification, of the cliques and coteries which ran the teaching of English literature in Britain and which secured for themselves all the best positions. Leavis himself often spoke of 'flank-rubbing', in respect of literary evaluation mostly but also of university administration; and because the metaphor is so striking, I particularly remember his references to those who were able to swim 'shoal-supported' to the shore. Yet after years of opposition to the ruling powers, he had established his own minor network of influence. At university rather than school level, this was perhaps much more evident abroad, as the experience of Jean-Marc Berthoud suggested; but there must have been some places at home where his name also carried weight, and where his support was therefore highly valuable. How fortunate I was to have had it was brought home to me much later by a friend and colleague who went to Cambridge only a few years after I did. A working class boy from Liverpool, he lived in St Edmond's, then a Catholic 'house of residence', while he was reading English at Fitzwilliam. For reasons not easy to explain, there were strong ties between Leavis and some of the priests at St Edmond's, as well as with other Catholic groups. They too may have felt beleaguered and it may be also that they had detected in his writing a whiff of that nostalgia for the pre-industrial many of them shared ('Ah, there's a donkey', exclaims the priest in a Catholic joke, 'this country must be Catholic'). Whatever the explanation, relations between Leavis and St Edmund's were close so that my friend found himself often having tea with him there, and then being invited back to the Leavises' house. When he decided to apply for a State Studentship he had received a sufficient number of encouraging signs from Leavis and felt he knew him well enough to request his support. He was asked who the other referees were and, on explaining that one was Raymond Williams, found the support denied. 'Oh don't be silly, Frank', Mrs Leavis apparently then said, 'if you won't do it, I will'. Excluding the idea that this was a protest on Leavis's part against my friend's patent Marxism, this is about the worst thing I have ever heard about him (and the best about his wife).

TWELVE

RESEARCH

T he topic I had chosen when I made my application for a State studentship was the reception of French literature in England during the
mid-nineteenth century. I think it had occurred to me when reading
Matthew Arnold and wondering what the state of play had been before he
came on the scene; but I suspect it was also designed to keep up my connection with France (and perhaps help me get back there). The first problem was
to find a supervisor, someone who, without necessarily being a nineteenth-
century specialist, would not be a liability in the poisonous atmosphere of
the Cambridge English Faculty. The year before, Ian Jack had written to the
TLS and criticised the inadequate scholarship of Leavisian graduate students.
Leavis had responded by withdrawing from graduate supervision entirely on
the grounds that it had become dangerous to be known as a pupil of his. The
ill-feeling was such that I was advised to find a supervisor who was more or
less acceptable to all camps and a natural choice was therefore Leo Salingar,
even though his speciality was Elizabethan drama. Salingar had moved from
extra-mural work to a fellowship at Trinity and would later publish a book on
Renaissance comedy, scholarly enough to have qualified for a *doctorat d'Etat*.
But in his earlier days he had reviewed a book for *Scrutiny* and was known to
be broadly sympathetic to Leavisian views.

The controversy which had elicited Ian Jack's letter to the *TLS* had also
brought from Leavis a substantial piece on further degrees in English in
which he had described the ideal research student as 'capable of proposing
for himself a sustained piece of work worth doing' so that 'a standing relation with a congenial senior to whom he could go now and then for criticism

and advice' was all the help he would need. Salingar was a cultivated man who knew French well, and he was certainly congenial. I experienced nothing but kindness and encouragement from him, although I felt I could have done with more criticism. I knew what I was doing – reading all the French novels, plays and poems which had made any kind of impression in Britain and then tracking quite how they were received, in the occasional book but chiefly in the major British periodicals – yet I easily lost sight of why I was doing it. The first thing I discovered was what to others must have been already familiar and obvious: how extraordinarily politicised most of these periodicals were. This was particularly evident in their treatment of French literature: twenty or even thirty years after the Napoleonic wars were over, the greater sexual explicitness of writers such as Balzac or George Sand was still being related back by their British critics to events in France during the early 1790s, and condemned or praised accordingly. For a majority of reviewers, the principal point to be made about writing over the Channel was that too much political freedom meant a lowering of standards in private life which French novels only too graphically illustrated. This state of affairs was easy to establish but I was in some doubt what more, having once established it, there might be to say. I was short on directing ideas and later used occasionally to think that things would have been different had I read English at Jesus, with Raymond Williams, rather than at Downing, although there were dangers in that solution also. The university I first worked in was in Australia and named after a man whose family motto was '*qui cherche trouve*'. This is, I suppose, 'seek and ye shall find' but I used to feel that mistranslated as 'you always find what you're looking for', it would provide the perfect banner under which research students in English could march. That would, however, only represent one end of a continuum which has at its other the danger of aimless accumulation. As I toiled on with my research, I began to feel it was like some long, arduous trek into what is sometimes called Australia's dead heart, in order to make absolutely certain it was no longer beating.

Long before I began struggling with problems of method, I was faced on my arrival back in Cambridge, not with the 'propaedeutic year' for which people like Ian Jack were then agitating, but a short, semi-compulsory induction course, elementary training in research. The rest of my university career would be punctuated by arguments about whether such courses were of any use. Since my memory of the one I took reduced itself to a few tips about how to use the library or construct a bibliography, matters that could be picked up in an hour or two and as one went along (I was after all working in the nineteenth not the fifteenth century), my view was always that they were not. But my resistance at the time was, I suspect, more instinctively ideological since I felt there were forces abroad which wanted to turn me into a scholar and that was a soft option I ought to resist as far as I could. Since that time, I have probably worked with many more colleagues who were anxious to be scholars than those who wanted to be above all critics. It must in part be a question of temperament. There are clearly lots of people who are happy to know things, even if it is only for the sake of knowing them, and love to be in libraries. The reverent hush, the leather-topped tables, the dull gold of the ancient books lining the walls ... all those familiar features of working in a university library like the one in Cambridge, including the sight of some famous old scholar shuffling his way to his accustomed seat, excite or perhaps rather soothe their senses. For me, on the other hand, the Cambridge 'UL' was much less a palace of learning than a comfortable prison. With its thick phallic tower ('this magnificent erection', the dignitary who opened it in the 1930s is supposed to have remarked), huge oblong windows, narrow and tessellated so that they seemed to have been barred against exit as well as entry, and a portentous flight of steps leading to its entrance, it was never a building in whose cavernous main reading rooms I felt comfortable. It is true that it was then and still is a largely open shelf library, so that I could hide away in one of the wings with row upon row of *The Edinburgh Review*, *The Quarterly*, *Blackwood's*, or *Fraser's* close by. That was an immense privilege and convenience, yet I was still glad to get out and into the fresh air, especially as what I found in these periodicals hardly confirmed the Leavises' belief that nineteenth-century literary journalism was far superior to what followed. Of course, I approve of libraries and deplore the way vice-chancellors have a tendency to make them the first stopping-place in the search for economies because the damage then done is not immediately noticeable; but I am nonetheless immensely grateful for the arrival of the internet.

Really serious effort I still equated at this time with critical reading. That engaged the whole structure of your thought and feeling, often leaving it painfully or embarrassingly exposed. To read a great book you had to be at your best and it took what I knew Lawrence had called 'hard, hard work' to come to 'real grips with one's imagination'. Although he was talking about writing rather than reading, it seemed relevant that Lawrence had gone on to describe how trying to ensure that his mood was appropriately 'deep and sincere', reminded him of St Lawrence on the gridiron saying, 'Turn me over, brothers, I am done enough on this side'. I knew that in many contexts literary scholarship was indispensable and that knowledge was always inextricably entangled with literary response; but I was more than usually aware of the temptation of assuming that, if the knowledge were increased, the quality of the response would automatically improve. When I began teaching, I became much more conscious than I had been of certain forms of ignorance which are disabling. There was the Japanese student puzzled about why, at the end of the wounded surgeon section in Eliot's 'East Coker', a Friday should be called 'good'; and very occasionally, someone had to be told that when Othello says that he will return incontinent, the word does not have the meaning it usually carries today. Discussing various exchanges in Shakespeare's comedies, I discovered that certain moments were incomprehensible unless a student was in possession of the elementary fact that, in Shakespeare's time, all the female parts were played by males. This is knowledge – cultural, linguistic, historical – of the most basic kind and which it can be assumed all reasonably educated readers possess. What else they might need is impossible to define so that the only generalisation which would seem to hold in this area is that information becomes more significant the further back in time one goes. Challenged with why he had never written on Chaucer, Leavis himself replied that, although he thought Chaucer was a great poet, writing about him would require a degree of specialist knowledge he did not feel he had.

Of all the areas of specialist knowledge, the one a Downing man would have least thought of pursuing was textual scholarship. Our interest was in the words on the page and not in how they got there (or whether they could reasonably be considered the right ones). Although I did not know it at the time, our attitude to editing had been encapsulated in several striking phrases that occur in the essay by Mrs Leavis called 'The Discipline of Letters: A sociological note'. This appeared in *Scrutiny* in 1943 and was a follow-up to her sympathetic review of a biography of A. C. Haddon, published in the journal's previous number. Haddon was the man who had established the study of anthropology in Cambridge, in spite of the university's cold indifference and refusal to advance his career. Her feeling that there was a strong parallel here with her husband can be glimpsed when she notes that Haddon was regarded as 'dangerous' by the university authorities and then adds 'for this reason no doubt a campaign of personal calumny and social ostracism was undertaken against him, as is usual in similar cases'. But it is perhaps at its clearest when, following a description of some of Haddon's difficulties in Cambridge, Mrs Leavis writes, 'The real burden fell on his wife, who had to raise a family under the most difficult conditions of financial and psychological strain'.

'The Discipline of Letters' seems to have been written because, soon after reading the Haddon biography, Mrs Leavis came across *The Letters of G. S. Gordon*, which presented a quite different picture. Here was a professor of English who had held a number of important posts in Oxford, including the most important one of Vice-Chancellor, without ever having written anything of note; but who had always had the right backers and got on well with those in power. For her he illustrated perfectly that fatal confusion in Oxbridge between social and intellectual distinction. Her treatment is scathing, with the odd flash of mordant wit. What in her view Gordon's letters principally showed is that the most important things in life are '(1) good mixing – a good man is one who likes a good dinner and knows the right people and (2) scholarship for its own sake'. 'We see that one corollary of the latter belief', she then goes on, 'is that the ability to edit a text is the only and sufficient test of academic fitness, hence the man who has edited any insignificant text is qualified to practice literary criticism and to direct literary studies'. Later on in the essay, Mrs Leavis exchanges irony for direct statement and claims that: 'the ability to edit texts and make piddling comments on them is no more qualification by itself for an English university post than a certificate of librarianship since it is an ability that can be readily acquired by quite stupid people with no interest in literature'. In the obituary she published in *The Cambridge Review* after Mrs Leavis's death, Muriel Bradbrook claimed that 'Queenie was the more masculine, Leavis the more indirect and feminine' of the couple. Certainly she is the more straightforward, sometimes crudely blunt, although what she says here still strikes me as broadly accurate, as long as the emphasis is allowed to fall on 'by itself'. 'Piddling' was perhaps not however a good idea since it inevitably, and no doubt deliberately, recalls Pope's reference to 'piddling Thibalds' in *The Epistle to Arbuthnot* and therefore the general consensus that many of the criticisms of Pope's edition of Shakespeare which were made by Thibald (or rather Theobald, as his name was usually spelt) were not at all piddling, but in fact well founded. And it was after all Theobald, the despised editor, who transformed an incomprehensible phrase in the Hostess's description of Falstaff's death in *Henry V* into the moving 'he babbled of green fields'.

My acquaintance with textual scholarship at this time was limited to struggling through those sections entitled 'The Text' in the introductions to the Arden editions of Shakespeare. Since that made me parasitic on someone else's hard labour, I have never been surprised that editors have often wanted to claim crucial importance for their work. Yet when dealing with texts of the nineteenth and twentieth centuries, I have rarely been convinced that the number of occasions on which editing has made a significant difference is all that great. As the Cambridge edition of D. H. Lawrence's works began to gather momentum, I was able to watch my friend Mark Kinkead-Weekes sweating over his edition of *The Rainbow* and even John Wiltshire, my companion in the tutorials with Mrs Leavis and a literary critic to his fingertips, eventually found himself editing *Mansfield Park*, also in a new Cambridge edition. I genuinely regret never having edited something myself (there was the possibility of a Lawrence text at one moment but it came to nothing). Perhaps only if I had done my time in the editorial galleys could I say with any authority that the logic which claims that preparing a text is either a necessary or sufficient qualification for talking about it critically is faulty, although it seems to me that the evidence is usually clear enough.

If textual scholarship, with its associated disciplines, was not an option for me as a research student, it is not surprising that I should have taken one of the more obvious, alternative paths, the one which led to cultural history. Judging by the books which appear, a majority of the Ph.D. theses now being written under the auspices of English could be labelled in this way. The emergence of new aspects of the discipline, such as feminist or post-colonial studies, has strengthened the trend, especially as both of these disciplines have the advantage of clear directing ideas. The almost total disappearance of research topics of a recognisable literary critical complexion has often struck me as a pity and I have sometimes been heard complaining that when a great novel or poem is used to support some generalisation about culture, the qualities which make it worth reading tend to be ignored. It has seemed to me also that the kind of cultural enquiry those trained in English sometimes undertake does not necessarily need for its exemplification texts taken from the old canon, and that indeed, because those texts tend to be unrepresentative, they can be a hindrance rather than a help. The problem I now see with these grumblings is not only that I attempted cultural history myself, but that this was the direction in which Leavis himself had clearly pointed. In the early 1940s, at a time when thought was already being given to a post-war world, he boldly proposed a reform of the Cambridge English Tripos. His 'Sketch for an "English School"' dealt only with the second, one year part of the degree and suggested that it should focus on the seventeenth century. Listing twenty-two topics, any one of which students might choose for the 'extended piece of writing' that would be part of a new, revolutionary examining system – the chief purpose of the old being 'to produce journalists' – he began with 'The background of religious history', 'Calvinism to Puritan individualism', 'Puritan to Nonconformist', before moving through eighteen others, none of which would seem to require the student to concentrate on the specifically literary aspects of particular texts. That kind of thing, his assumption was, would have been dealt with in the first part of the Tripos and already left students fully qualified literary critics. It is as such that they would, in dealing with subjects very firmly in the domain of cultural history, or of history *tout court*, bring to bear the requisite 'tact and delicacy of interpretation, an awareness of complexities, and a sense of the subtle ways in which, in a concrete cultural situation, the spiritual and the material are related'.

Just like many proponents of cultural history today, Leavis appears to assume that literary critical training was not something that needed to be extended into more advanced study, but that once the right ground work had been established, the student could be relied on to go on reading in the same attentive and discriminating fashion as before. Yet he seems to me to have himself illustrated one of the dangers of the model he was proposing in his treatment of Dickens. If in *The Great Tradition* he had chosen *Hard Times* as the most successful of all Dickens's novels, it was because he felt it was much more tightly organised and focussed than the others. Discussing James's *Portrait of a Lady*, he says that 'it is all intensely significant. It offers no largesse of irrelevant life; its vitality is wholly that of art'; and he believed he could make similar claims for *Hard Times*. Yet the appeal of this short novel for him was clearly also that its target was Utilitarianism, the Benthamite approach to life. As he became increasingly preoccupied with tracing the origins of those 'technologico-Benthamite' tendencies which he felt were destroying his own culture, and which he found personified in C. P. Snow, he also became more concerned to celebrate those people who had fought against these tendencies in the past. It is not surprising therefore that he should have again identified Dickens as such a person when he decided that works like *Dombey and Son* and *Little Dorrit* were even greater, in their length and complexity, than *Hard Times*. But reading *Little Dorrit* as an inspired criticism of social evils which had continued to grow since it was written, also committed Leavis, his criteria being what they were, to regarding it, not only as Dickens's 'greatest book', but also a novel in which there was 'wonderfully close organic unity' and 'a unifying and controlling life'. Also as one against which 'there are no large qualifications to be urged'. Readers who struggle with *Little Dorrit*'s absurdly melodramatic plot or groan when they realise they are in for another session with Dickens's honest working folk, in the shape of the Plornishes, could hardly agree with that. Even the undoubted comic success of Flora Finching, rightly made much of by Leavis, would surely be even more successful if she appeared on fewer occasions. The truth for many is that *Little Dorrit* is like any other great Dickens novel, miraculous in parts (and Leavis is excellent in showing which these parts are), but downright tedious in others. His inclination to deny its shortcomings, as well as play down how much stronger a descriptive term one would need to describe its treatment of certain sexual matters (not so nauseating in *Little Dorrit* as in *Dombey*, but bad enough), derives I think from his determination to use the novel as an item in his indictment of forces in Dickens's society which he saw as still operative in his own. He always said that he did not believe in any exclusively literary values and that the reading of great literature naturally led into thinking about society, past and present. But that does not mean that literary values should be sacrificed in order to facilitate such thinking. In Leavis's later treatment of Dickens, it seems to me that literary criticism sometimes falls prey to cultural history so that any Leavisian who felt he could detect that same process going on elsewhere, might well have to mutter, 'If gold rust, what then shall iron do'.

THIRTEEN

THEORY

M y Ph.D. was a mistake for which I only have myself to blame, but at least it got me back to Paris. I spent the middle of the three years of the State studentship in a fourth floor flat from the windows of which one could see the side wall of Saint-Sulpice. Opposite the façade of this church, and across Saint-Sulpice square, was the town hall of the sixth arrondissment where I was married. The official who performed the ceremony was a portly man with a wide tri-colour sash diagonally displayed across his ample chest and lower regions. His splendid appearance increased the sympathy I already felt for the secular, anti-clerical tradition in France (*écrasez l'infâme*). My future wife's parents claimed that her already ailing grandfather would die unless she and I complemented the civil formalities with a benediction in a church and we agreed to this very much on the same principles once espoused by Henry of Navarre. I was glad that this religious service did not take place in Saint-Sulpice, convenient although that would have been, since it has always struck me as one of the ugliest churches in Paris.

It would be hard to think of a more privileged place for students to live than the Saint-Sulpice area. We inherited the flat from a Cambridge researcher and his wife, and the rent was very low because the whole building was undergoing extensive renovation. At one point during the year water dripped from above onto our bed and at another, much more extended one, the landlord's builders demolished our bathroom and toilet. The inconvenience of this second episode was considerable, but the flat was only a few minutes' walk uphill to the Luxembourg Gardens and only a few hundred yards downhill to the Odéon metro and the centre of the Latin Quarter. From there, you could move left into Saint-Germain-des-Près and past those cafés, *Les Deux Magots* or *Le Flore*, where it was rumoured Sartre and his friends still occasionally hung out; or right into the Boulevard Saint-Michel and student life at its most visible and lively. Every morning I would go neither right nor left but straight on down towards the river and cross the Seine by the Pont des Arts. I would then make my way via the Comédie-Française and the Palais-Royal to the Bibliothèque nationale. This was like a topographical demonstration of bathos since the French National Library was at that time – it has been relocated since – in a miserably dilapidated condition. Not that I minded this much. What made it an unpleasant place to work was the attitude of the staff. Whether it was that they were very badly paid, poorly managed or deliberately recruited to deter researchers from handling too many old books, they were almost uniformly surly, rude and unco-operative. In the Cambridge University Library, the librarians tended to be a little aloof and had subtle ways of reminding you of how privileged you were to be there; but they were always helpful and polite. In the BN, as it was known, anyone requesting a book – no open shelves there – was made to feel like Oliver Twist asking for more.

My time at the BN would have been unhappy had I not met a group of British Ph.D. students with whom I regularly had a cheap lunch in one of the local restaurants. Although they were largely from Oxbridge, they were uniformly students of French and their intellectual background was therefore very different from mine. As far as I remember, their reasons for being in the library were sound in that it was a place where they could consult texts not available elsewhere. My own presence was justified by having to check up on the odd writer who had been noticed in England in the 1830s and '40s and then sunk into obscurity, or the occasional journal article of relevant interest; but for a good deal of my time I was reading writers whom I could have read at home. The author who interested me more than any other was Stendhal but he had barely made an impression over the Channel, despite several British contacts and what he would have claimed was a friendship with Lord Byron. Stendhal famously predicted that his writings would not begin to be properly appreciated before 1880. Since that would turn out to be true in France, it is no surprise that, before this date, they were very little known in Britain.

Balzac was the writer who mattered most for the British (poems and plays concerned them much less than novels). I still cannot quite understand why it was that I decided I ought therefore to read the whole of the *Comédie Humaine* (ninety odd stories and novels in total). I would probably be flattering myself if I said it was because I had been looking at some of the so-called phenomenological criticism of people like George Poulet and Jean

Starobinski, who insisted on the importance of working with the whole body of a writer's work. The more likely explanation for my mad scheme was that at some point, and perhaps because of my contacts with the other research students, I had been bitten by the bug of comprehensiveness. If you were going to study a particular writer, then you ought surely to have read all he or she had ever produced? It seemed obvious enough and I had certainly, in my enthusiasm for Stendhal, read more or less everything he had written. But that was a different case. He was the author of only three published novels and had otherwise written a wide variety of texts, nearly each one of which revealed a different aspect of his literary personality. Balzac, on the other hand, was more of a piece. If you had read half of dozen of his novels, including, for example, *Le père Goriot*, *Eugénie Grandet* or the splendidly grotesque *La Cousine Bette*, then it seemed to me *later* that you had learnt pretty much everything you needed to know about him as a writer. Plodding through all the fiction he wrote could only turn you into a specialist and offer a further demonstration of how discontinuous with the alert teaching of literature research could be. It would also be likely to deaden your sensibilities and thereby be not only discontinuous with that future task, but also a disqualification for it. Of all the Balzac I then read in the BN, I now remember precious little. The only image that has always stayed in my mind is of *La Cousine Bette*'s Baron Hulot still pursuing women in his decrepit old age, obsession, or what an English reader might think of as Jonsonian humour, being one of the pathological conditions Balzac renders best.

Poulet and Starobinski were names to conjure with in those days and they are a reminder to me that a critical revolution was brewing then which would transform the teaching of English literature both at home and abroad. Since the principal figures involved were French, and not translated into English until the 1970s, I was in a position to steal a march on many of my contemporaries. That I did not do so could hardly be ascribed to good nature. The one then current fashion among literary people in which I did participate was psychoanalysis. I read at this time a great deal of Freud, in both French and English, and particularly his case histories. I was attracted by his remarkable skill in handling narrative and his ability to meet an objection just minutes after it had first occurred to you. It seemed to me that he often displayed, in describing his patients, a psychological shrewdness very much akin to that found in the great novelists or playwrights; and I was regularly left open-mouthed by his fiendish ingenuity. But there were questions of temperament which appealed to me also. I responded above all, for example, to his pessimism, memorably encapsulated in his claim that the chief aim of his treatment was to transform hysterical misery into common unhappiness.

None of this had any necessary connection with psychoanalysis itself. I engaged with its theory, as anyone who read Freud must, but I could never get rid of the feeling that much of it was far-fetched. At the beginning of his case history of Dora, a text I admired and would eventually write about, he describes how he asked a fellow specialist for an opinion of the theory of hysteria put forward in that work and was bluntly told that it was 'an unjustifiable generalisation of conclusions which might hold good for a few cases'. Freud mentions this view with scorn, but it was more or less my own. That it is to say that although I believed that even the Oedipus complex, or perhaps especially the Oedipus complex, might be a useful analytic tool in certain circumstances, I could not accept the idea of its universal validity, just as I could not work out why, as I later found Frank Cioffi had put it, 'a theory about the pathogenic centrality of the boy's sexual desire for his mother had been inspired by women's false memories of having been seduced by their fathers'. This scepticism was a poor preparation for an encounter with Jacques Lacan, whose *Ecrits* had only recently appeared. He offered none of the more obviously literary compensations of Freud and I struggled hard with his rewriting of the Freudian topography in terms of post-Saussurean linguistics, both then and subsequently. I could see that the mirror stage, for example, was an ingenious way of explaining the radical uneasiness of our presence in the world; but it never struck me as the only way and I found the personality which emerged from the writing so disagreeable that Lacan was at the very bottom of my list of persons to turn to, should I ever feel the need of psychoanalysis myself. Try as I might, I could not see how he was relevant to the novels, plays or poems which interested me, or to anything I might want to say about them.

I bought Lacan's *Ecrits* from one of several splendid bookshops on the Boulevard Saint-Michel and it was there that I also acquired my first copies of Roland Barthes: *Le degré zéro de l'écriture*, *Mythologies* and *Sur Racine*. Earlier I said that I have very little feeling for books as material objects, but the exceptions were these and later works by Barthes in the *Editions du Seuil*. As he became more famous he was able to publish shorter texts in this format, with bigger print, so that his book on photography (*La Chambre Claire*), with its wonderful expanses of white around the large lettering, became my model of what a book should ideally look like, especially at a time when English academic publishers were cramming more and more words onto the enlarged pages, and thinner paper, of their books. With my eyesight weakening, I became a propagandist for this model until someone publishing one of my own books rather irritably told me that she was considering offering it to the public with a free white stick (an addition, I ought to have pointed out, that would not help the poorly sighted to read the print better).

The pleasure I still get from handling a book by Barthes is partly physical but also a testimony to the fact that he enthralled me in a way none of the other leading figures in the 'theory' revolution did, or would. I relished his ability to transfer his analytic powers to popular culture; when his book on Racine provoked a backlash from the academic establishment, I made silent comparisons (without too much investigation of the matter!) with the storm Leavis had created in his criticism of Milton; and I felt enlightened by his demonstration of how many practices we think of as 'natural' are culturally conditioned. I enjoyed all his work, with the exception of *S/Z*, his post-structuralist analysis of a short story by Balzac. In general, what I liked about all French critical writing was a passion for establishing distinctions, making categories, taxonomising. Later, when I was trying to think about auto-biography, I would become keen on the work of Philippe Lejeune, who offered a definition of the form which attracted me by its precision even though, in claiming that no autobiography could ever be written in verse, he excluded the one on which I happened to be working (Wordsworth's *Prelude*). Barthes had this taxonomising habit in spades, but in *S/Z*, under the influence of the Russian Formalists and the new linguistics, it seemed to me to have gone berserk and produced the only one of his works which I thought boring. Very different was the later *Roland Barthes par Roland Barthes*, a work which impressed me as so subtly aware of the problems of literary self-presentation that I published an essay in its praise. Re-reading Barthes's text recently, I was struck by how many references to contemporary theorists it contains (in my essay I dealt only with those to Lacan), and wondered therefore if I had not read him rather as I had Freud: for what might be called his more exclusively 'literary' value. If that was the case, it would not be surprising given that Barthes was not only the best stylist among the new French avant-garde critics but the only one of them whose chief interest was literature (his devotion to Proust, explicit in *Roland Barthes par Roland Barthes*, is apparent everywhere).

If I needed a justification for the way I may have read Barthes it would be that, although his hostility to authority or what he called the 'doxa' – in language, politics or sexual behaviour – was clearly genuine and deep-seated, he was also something of an intellectual dandy, often playing with fashion-able ideas just for the fun of it. An implicit admission of this comes at the beginning of the book on photography where after some fancy footwork in pursuit of an objective, proto-scientific analysis of the photographic image, Barthes abandons theory and decides that he will simply describe various photographs to which he is attached and try to explain the effect they have on him. He justifies this procedure by adding that he has always wanted to 'open a discussion with [his] moods', not so that he can defend them, and still less so as to 'fill the scene of the text with [his] individuality'; but on the contrary so that he can offer that individuality as a contribution to 'a science of the subject'. All this is expressed with Barthes's characteristic finesse yet the risk he obviously takes is of giving the impression of a rationalisation: of wanting to talk about himself and needing an excuse to make that respectable. Certainly he is in a long line of memoir writers who would like to feel that their self-absorption – and what author of a memoir is not (like this one) to some extent self-absorbed – can make a contribution to the general good. For me, a contribution is certainly what Barthes made, as much or even more when he abandoned any close adherence to a formal *science* of the subject (such as is offered by Lacanian psychoanalysis), as when he was eclectically pursuing the traditional spectre of self-knowledge. And, after all, one of the first and best of his essays was on La Rochefoucauld.

The nature of my encounter with Barthes might help to explain why it was that, unlike many of my contemporaries, I was not much taken by Foucault and even less by Derrida, both of whom had published important books in 1966. Their interests seemed a long way from mine and I did not feel equipped to deal with their more obviously philosophical approach. In France, philosophy was and is the queen of the humanities. Most of those who eventually went on to teach literature had taken the *bac de philo*, the baccalaureate in which philosophy was the principal subject. One particularly striking consequence of this was someone like Sartre, the author of important novels and plays but also of a major philosophical treatise. There was no equivalent figure in Britain. No teaching of philosophy went on in my grammar school and I did not have the advantage of the friend mentioned earlier – the one from Fitzwilliam who often had tea with the Leavises – since he had once been a candidate for the Catholic priesthood and had cut his philosophical teeth on chunks of Duns Scotus and Thomas Aquinas. If this left me with a defect, it was one there was little encouragement to remedy in Downing. The ambition of Leavis was after all to establish *English* as the centre of any Humanities faculty and he was suspicious of the potentially damaging effects of a philosophical training on literary criticism. They had appeared to him evident in 1937 when he had replied to the criticisms of *Revaluation* made by René Wellek, who was really a historian of ideas but whom Leavis treated as a philosopher (the title of his reply was 'Literary Criticism and Philosophy'). Wellek's complaint that Leavis ought to have been more systematic in explaining what his criteria for good poetry were and that, in his readings of Blake, Wordsworth and Shelley, he took too little account of 'Romantic' philosophy, were in themselves for Leavis an illustration of 'how difficult it is to be a philosopher and a literary critic at the same time'. When he responded, it was not so much by tackling the fundamental issues implicit in Wellek's essay, but by first of all showing – in a fine passage

– how alien to any proper engagement with literature is the idea of bringing to bear on a poem from the outside a 'norm' or previously held set of values; and by then illustrating how easy it is to misread poetry by focussing too much on the ideas of authors, or those of their age. The episode seems to have confirmed in Leavis a distrust of philosophers interfering in literary matters and, much later in his career, he would declare himself highly sceptical about the usefulness of seminars on Wittgenstein's linguistic philosophy for students of English.

There is enough hostility to philosophy in many of Leavis's writings to justify the title of his last, posthumous collection of essays, *The Critic as Anti-Philosopher;* and yet that gives a false impression of him as some kind of philosophical ignoramus. His concept of language as the medium into which we are born, and which conditions both our consciousness and what we are able to say, was a sophisticated one, broadly Wittgensteinian in direction. In practising his trade he was fully aware that he was continually coming across problems which have philosophical implications – the relation of language to experience, for example, or of information to aesthetic response – and displayed a skill in negotiating or skirting round these which, for at least one Cambridge philosopher (Michael Tanner), was indicative of 'a first-rate philosophical intelligence'. Towards the end of his career, in order to meet the charge that literary criticism was just a number of individuals airing their personal opinions, he developed a notion of 'the third realm' which begins to sound very much like philosophy. This realm is for him 'that which is neither merely personal nor public in the sense that it can be brought into the laboratory and pointed to' and, in speaking of it, Leavis is deploying the same ontological classification as Simmel when he talks of 'a mental category ... which is deep rooted and not easily described by traditional concepts ... a third something in man, beyond his individual subjectivity and the logical objective thinking which is universally convincing'; or Husserl when, in his fifth Cartesian Meditation, he claims that, for those who belong to the same cultural community, all cultural objects possess 'an experiential sense of thereness-for-everyone'. Yet if this last similarity had been pointed out to Leavis, it would not have convinced him that his own students, with all they already had on their plate, would benefit from reading Husserl, or indeed his pupil Heidegger, whose influence on many of the new French critics was even more powerful.

One of the more virulent of those who wrote to *The Spectator* after the Richmond lecture referred contemptuously to the 'Leavis tribe of logical positivists'. Although this is in general an absurd characterisation, it is true that there was at Downing in my time an impatience with whatever was felt to be too general or abstract, not dissimilar to that of the early verificationists. In our supervisions, we were continually being asked to explain what we meant and provide examples, and there was therefore a certain continuity between the model of critical writing held up before us and Leavis's famous criticism of Shelley in *Revaluation* for his 'weak grasp upon the actual'. (It is to the earlier Leavis we looked not the later cultural critic who is certainly not shy of generalities.) The pedagogic consequences were not the best preparation for opening Heidegger, or any other philosopher in the German idealist tradition, and for trying to see one's way through the flurry of abstract nouns and technical terms so often found there. Not that this could be anything more than a partial explanation of my failure to make much of Foucault, whose book on madness I enjoyed reading but whose possible relevance to my own work escaped me. That Derrida did offer an approach to literary texts, one that appeared to involve seizing them by their most unobtrusive features and flipping them over (as it were) to reveal a hidden structure, was something I only realised, and rejected, much later. But neither of these two had an impact on me at all comparable to Barthes's, a fact that I am here attributing to educational nurture but one that may just as well have been the responsibility of my own nature. One does what one can.

FOURTEEN

AUSTRALIA

As the end of my three year studentship approached, my Ph.D. was still far from finished. This was a common situation at the time when many graduate students used their grant money for the acquisition of a more general education and treated the writing of an actual thesis as a side-show. In a way which would be impossible for their equivalents today (when the authorities are much more anxious to see an 'outcome' for their money), they indulged themselves in a great deal of reading which, from the point of view of finishing the Ph.D. on time, could accurately be described as ill-directed. If they were like me, only later and as they began teaching did they begin always to read with a distinct purpose in mind (a class, lecture, an article) until they eventually found themselves unable to pick up any book without some lurking ulterior motive. 'Why am I reading this?' is a question I don't remember asking myself very often in those days. Perhaps I took some bogus comfort from a striking remark made by Henry James, which was sometimes held up to us. This occurs in his 1872 review of a *History of English Literature*, after James has imagined its author, Hippolyte Taine, deciding to fulfil his commission handsomely by devoting to it five or six years and spending an equivalent number of months in England. 'He has performed his task', James writes, 'with a vigour proportionate to this sturdy resolve; but in the nature of the case his treatment of the subject lacks that indefinable quality of spiritual initiation which is the tardy consummate fruit of a wasteful, purposeless, passionate sympathy'. This is well put and says something important about Taine's brisk, businesslike manner; but to apply it to the many wasteful, purposeless hours I spent as a research student would be too flatteringly optimistic.

The approaching end of the scholarship meant that I needed a job and I therefore began applying for one. In comparison once more with the situation today, when several articles, a doctorate completed and a book on the way is the going rate, I had desperately little to offer. My only publication was I think a long review of Leon Edel's biography of James in *Delta*, something of a Downing house journal in that period; but such was the number of jobs then available, and the lower expectation from candidates (publications not being regarded as so important), I fairly quickly secured two interviews. One was at Warwick, which did not go well, and the other at Cardiff, which went even worse. It was thought by one or two of my friends that I would have a good chance at Cardiff because a once quite prominent Scrutineer, G. D. Klingopulos, worked there. But I don't remember ever seeing let alone meeting him in Wales, and if he did put in a word for me it had no effect. It strikes me now that my friends were naïve to assume that the Leavis world was still homogenous. Just as I was beginning my research, there had been that almighty quarrel between Leavis and those admirers of his such as John Newton who had recently been involved in founding *The Cambridge Quarterly*. I regarded the details of this dispute as being well above my pay level but I knew that, after the appointment of H. A. Mason to the F. R. Leavis Lectureship, matters had not been improved by the publication in *The Cambridge Quarterly* of an article by Newton entitled '*Scrutiny*'s failure with Shakespeare'. The consequence of the quarrel was a house divided against itself so it could be that, in Klingopulous's view, I fell on the wrong side of the divide. On the other hand, there were plenty of sound, objective reasons why I should not have been appointed in Cardiff and Klingopulous may have had nothing to do with the decision at all.

It does not do to wonder too much about these things and at the time I certainly did not give them a second thought. In her stinging review of the letters of George Gordon, Mrs Leavis pays a lot of attention to his teacher and patron, Walter Raleigh (or Sir Walter Raleigh as he became, adding to the confusion). A professor of English at Liverpool, Glasgow and then Oxford, he was a gifted but cynical individual who once said that, if he were accused on Judgement Day of teaching literature, he would plead that he had never believed in it and, anyway, it had fed his wife and children. That is no doubt a deplorable remark but Mrs Leavis excoriates him for another which seems to me more reasonable. Invited to Glasgow to receive what he described as a ridiculous honorary degree, he said 'I call it ridiculous because I have been in the kitchen where these things are cooked'. Much later in life, I often found myself in the kitchen from which university appointments emerge.

In my experience, the vast majority of colleagues discharged their duties as conscientiously and fairly as possible; but in the nature of the case there were trivial details that tipped the balance, narrow victories or defeats, and the occasional manifestation of mindless prejudice or *parti pris*. The ignorance of just how these things are cooked, which I along with the other candidates for the posts in Cardiff and Warwick enjoyed, is therefore a largely happy one, as much for the beneficiaries of the system as its victims.

I would have gone on applying for a job, after these two early set-backs, had I not suddenly and quite unexpectedly been offered one. The ultimate source was the same connections in South Africa I had encountered in Jean-Marc Berthoud. An academic from that country had migrated to Australia and was setting up an English department in a new university in Melbourne. He was on a recruiting mission in England and asked one of my supervisors at Downing whether he could recommend anybody. I was invited to apply to La Trobe, as the new university was called, on the understanding that I would probably be appointed, sight unseen. The difference between being offered a job and having to compete for one is so great that I was delighted by the prospect, as was my wife even though one of her relations was later to say that Australia was where French people go just before they take off for the moon. The episode brought out again the pros and cons of being a Leavisite. There were very many places where it was as disadvantageous as being a Jew in Elizabethan England; but that was not always the case. I have said that the minor spheres of influence operated chiefly abroad and I had another, different glimpse of them when, after two years in Australia, my wife and I decided we would convert what was the summer break at my university into Christmas in France and flew back to Europe via Singapore. In charge of the English department in the English-speaking university there, was D. J. Enright and on his staff was one Downing man together with a Sri Lankan who had imbibed Leavisian principles under E. F. C. Ludowyck at the University of Colombo. During the Second World War and shortly after, Enright had written a number of important pieces for *Scrutiny*. The Leavises were rightly proud of having continued at that time to pay serious attention to German literature and Enright was the person they chiefly turned to for the task. After the war he held a series of teaching posts in both the East and Europe before landing up in Singapore in 1960. By the time I met him, there was a drive by the Singaporean government to replace expatriates with locally born university staff and he was being subjected to all kinds of petty restrictions and indignities in order to persuade him to move on.

We stayed in Singapore longer than we meant to because, as the plane in which we were leaving was taxiing to take off, the pilot had a heart attack and we had to wait forty-eight hours for a replacement to be flown out. There was considerable gloom among the expatriates there at the prospect of having to leave the country and an end-of-empire feeling in the staff club where some quite heavy drinking went on. Enright did more than his fair share of this, but he had a remarkable constitution and was always able to get up early in the morning in order to attend conscientiously to his professorial duties, or write another review. He was unusual for a Leavisite in being a prominent and successful literary journalist, and also a poet of enough distinction to have been included with Larkin, Amis, Davie and others in a grouping known in the 1950s as 'the Movement'. At Downing there had been precious little encouragement for writing poetry. After recognising that he had over-valued the work of Ronald Bottrall, Leavis came to feel that there had been no poet of any real value after Eliot and there hung in the Downing air that passage from 'The Function of Criticism at the Present Time' in which Arnold says that, although creative writing is 'the great proof of being alive', criticism itself can give a 'joyful sense of creative activity; a sense which a man of insight and conscience will prefer to what he might derive from a poor starved, fragmentary, inadequate creation. And at some epochs no other creation is possible'.

These words were seriously inhibiting but Enright had taken no notice of them. He was strong willed but also, as I learnt later when I got to know him well, warm-hearted, loyal and full of integrity. His one failing in my eyes was that, once settled in the pub with a pint, he could prove very reluctant to discuss literary matters. The only explanation I had for this was a fear of sounding pretentious. His Irish Catholic father was a postman who had died from lung cancer in his early 50s ('without benefit of smoking', as his son put it), and he had been brought up in Leamington Spa in comparative poverty: 'We had to keep our coal out at the back', he once wrote, 'They wouldn't give us a bath'. This background seems to have left him with a suspicion of intellectual life among the middle classes which never quite went away. It may have been some such associated scruples which meant that, when he left Singapore, he did not look for a job in an English university, or take one in America where he certainly had influential contacts, but instead, after a period as an editor of *Encounter*, went to work for Chatto and Windus (an appropriate berth given that Chatto was Leavis's publisher). He retired from there on a very small pension having spent (as far as I could gather) whatever money he had brought back from Singapore on a flat in Wandsworth – the top half of a modest suburban house. When I knew him he was always hard up and once showed me ruefully the complicated form he had to complete in order to apply for help from the Royal Literary Fund. That he had meanwhile been awarded the Queen's medal for poetry (a rare honour) only confirms the accuracy of Ezra Pound's Mr Nixon who, in 'Hugh Selwyn Mauberley', says

'And give up verse, my boy / There's nothing in it'. Enright was a proud man so that applying to the Literary Fund was a necessity which would not have been made less painful by my reminding him that D. H. Lawrence had had to do the same during the First World War. A sign of his integrity was that at around this time he told the editor of the *New York Review of Books* that he no longer wanted to be sent anything by them. Much of his small income came from casual reviewing and the Americans paid better than anyone. But, as he explained to me, they always wanted at least 3000 words and the books he received were never worth that. I might have thought then what a pity it was that the authors of all those interminable contributions to the *Quarterly* or *Edinburgh* reviews, which I had been obliged to read, had not shown the same compunction.

Meeting Enright was well in the future when we first set out for Australia. My new employer offered either economy aeroplane tickets or first class travel by boat. It seemed a simple choice to make and we boarded P.&O.'s *Canberra* sometime in January 1968. Travelling first-class was a strange experience. We were paired in the restaurant with a couple who always dressed for dinner. For half the trip the husband put on a regulation black smoking jacket and bow tie but then at one moment, which consisted I gathered in 'crossing the line', suddenly and disconcertingly appeared in an all-white version of the same uniform. They were nice enough people but elderly, as was the over-whelming majority of the passengers in first-class (my wife complained that those in the rest of the boat appeared to be having much more fun). Prominent among them was a large number of insurance widows who spent their time drinking at the bar and flirting with the stewards almost everyone of whom, as far as I could see, was gay. Despite a deadly 'entertainments officer', and elaborate menus which usually turned out to describe food more interesting to read about than eat, I found myself bored to death. We were unlucky in that the Suez canal was still then closed so that we had to sail round via Cape Town to Perth, with only two stops on the way. Much later in life I devised a way of adding to my contentment by using odd moments to draw up a list of luxuries (caviar, tickets for the Wimbledon final, a sports car) which I could never afford but would not want anyway. A cruise was at the very top. The best thing about it was that it gave me the ideal opportunity to read Richardson's *Clarissa*. This is a very great book but also a very long one, only likely to be more widely read when more people take boat trips to Australia.

The last time I was in Melbourne there were hoardings describing it as the world's most 'liveable' city. I can well believe it. There are some fine new buildings in the centre, it is full of cultural amenities and everywhere you go there are cafes and restaurants which reflect the many diverse nationalities that have come into the area during the last thirty or forty years. In the late 1960s it was a different story and a preponderance of Victorian gothic architecture made me feel that it was like Manchester by the sea – except that the sea was nowhere to be seen and you had to travel many miles to find one of those surf beaches for which Australia was famous. There was a strong drinking culture which the government had tried to control by closing the pubs at six. This meant that at 5.30, in expectation of people finishing work, glasses would be lined up on the bar and then filled with a hosepipe in order to save time. For the first week we were lodged in a dingy hotel in a even dingier suburb which did not endear itself to me by being called Preston. When I went to get a drink for us I found myself in a huge room like a cattle market, with sawdust on the floor, no women, and crowds of very tough looking, sweaty Australians in singlets. We needed the drink because we had arrived in a heat wave. At one point the temperature reached 106 degrees Fahrenheit and there were stories in the papers of £10 English migrants (that is how much it cost them to come), who had got off their plane, felt the heat, and immediately made their way back home again.

The temperature soon moderated, we found decent temporary accommodation and, after a rough start, not helped by most of our luggage having travelled on to Sydney (a consequence, my wife believed, of our not having tipped the stewards handsomely enough), began to enjoy and appreciate Australia. My university was called La Trobe because that was the name of a former governor of Victoria with French ancestry and that family motto of *qui cherche trouve*. The campus was a long way out of the city, on a site which was still being developed and therefore gave the impression of having been only recently rescued from the bush. In one of those juxtapositions also found all over the United States, it was in a spot known as Bundoora (an aboriginal word) but cheek by jowl with a village called Heidelberg. A long way from Cambridge and Leavis, one would have thought, yet that was far from being true. When I arrived, the Australian world of English Studies was still suffering the after-shocks of the great Sydney split. A young lecturer called Sam Goldberg, who paradoxically enough was best known as the author of an excellent book on Joyce, had formed in Melbourne a group of keen Leavis enthusiasts. When he was appointed to the chair in Sydney, he vigorously set about reforming the English department there on Leavisian lines. The resistance he met, and the anger which ensued, led to the establishment of two quite different degree paths for students and a division of the teaching staff into two rival camps. My professor had recently taught in Sydney and was called Derick Marsh. Though his appointment of me demonstrated that he had nothing against Leavisites, he had joined the anti-Goldberg faction. I never knew the reasons for this but imagined it had a lot to do with his background in South Africa where he had been a friend of Alan Paton and where his opposition to apartheid had earned him three months in prison. Goldberg was a dynamic individual but he was also authoritarian in manner, and likely to get up the nose of an instinctive liberal like Derick Marsh. The son of a farmer and a good enough fast bowler to have been twelfth man for Natal against the English touring test team, he was remarkably genial. The only time I saw him seriously disturbed was when he spotted a student tape-recording one of his lectures. Memories of being spied on in South Africa must have come back to him and he lost his temper.

Derick Marsh was a 'close reader' but the aspect of Leavis's teaching which probably most appealed to him was the insistence on the moral seriousness of all great literature. Without being completely at one with him on that score, I found his attitude to books very like mine and it did not surprise me that he had not only appointed me but was also welcoming to various of Goldberg's former admirers who came over to Melbourne from Sydney. At the same time he had clearly set out to be eclectic and in his liberal way had appointed one or two teachers with an Oxonian scholarly bent, as well as Americans to whom the name of Leavis meant nothing at all. We all got on reasonably well and he was a professor whom I admired and enjoyed working for. Setting up a new department was exciting and there were fierce debates about curricula which never spiralled out of control. A good number of the staff members were local and very welcoming. They had mostly been educated in Melbourne University and knew their way around a particularly attractive, semi-bohemian adjacent part of the city called Carlton (still one of the few places in the world I would prefer to live), full of nineteenth-century houses with wrought iron balconies. One or two of these locals were involved in an experimental theatre called La Mama, in homage to the one in New York, and introduced me to a lively cultural scene. When I think of how friendly they all were, I am struck by the strong reasons they had for being the opposite. In the first place, I was one of the imported poms taking up jobs which they might reasonably have thought ought to have been all theirs. In the second, they were mostly of Irish Catholic origin and had grown up in a milieu where there was a visceral hatred of the British. Perhaps they took a secret and unconscious revenge by ruining my health with midday visits to the local pub and weekend barbecues where charred, carcinogenic lumps of meat were washed down with cheap flagons of red wine (the epithet is transposable). When I think of the happiness of this time I find its explanation in the way the warmth we met everywhere, the easy-going friendliness of Australian social life, and the (for us) unfamiliar beauty of the countryside, was combined with the excitement of a first job, being young and having no parental responsibilities. In a couple of visits to Melbourne since, I have been able to see how the lives of colleagues who were with me in those early days have developed: what kind of houses they eventually bought, how their work conditions altered, or what they were able to make of the changing political and cultural climate. This has offered some sense of how our own lives would have been had we stayed in Australia and an apparent qualification therefore to the usual futility of counter-factual thinking. But of course there are so many variables between their situation and what ours could have become that trying to imagine what might have been is just as pointless as all efforts in that direction usually are. In the television show *Who wants to be a millionaire* contestants who have won a certain sum are asked whether they want to retain what they have or risk either losing or doubling it by trying to answer another question. If they plumb for retention, they are told what the question they declined to answer was and therefore know immediately how things would have been had they made a different choice. The occasions on which the outcomes of choices in life can be known in a similar way are very rare indeed.

FIFTEEN

SHAKESPEARE, STENDHAL AND JAMES SMITH

The contentment we felt in Australia was compounded by our finding an exceptional place to live. This was in what can only be called a village (although the word seems inappropriate), then on the very edge of Melbourne's continuing expansion into the surrounding bush. We met there an old Australian who wanted to rent a house he had built himself. It was a simple, single-storied affair, but it stood on a hill from where there were no other buildings in sight, and was surrounded by about an acre of land. At the bottom of the hill, just beyond our entrance posts, was a stream and a track known as Gold Memorial Road. The memorial in question celebrated the first gold strike in the area and, while we were living there, people would still occasionally turn up to pan the stream, with very modest results. The house had a primitive wood-burning kitchen range for cooking but the landlord took pity on my wife and installed an electric stove. Water came from a tank outside which he warned us not to jump into, should we find ourselves caught in a bush-fire. If we did, he explained, we would be boiled like an egg. We gained some sense of why this should be so when, in the colder season, we put sodden eucalyptus branches on our open fire and saw how quickly they released their petrol and exploded into flame. When a bush fire did run through the village, it avoided our hill but not a friend's house lower down which it reduced to a few bits of blackened, twisted metal from the washing machine.

Living where we did meant that we could keep a dog. Otto was a collie/ German shepherd cross we had as a puppy but never managed to train properly. His finest hour came one very wet day when we were surprised to see a four-by-four, too shiny and big to belong to any of our friends, making its way very slowly up the curves in our stony path. Out of it stepped two spruce looking men from Utah whom our dog greeted in his usual friendly way by putting his muddy paws all over their smart new suits. The ensuing discussion confirmed that elementary principle of literary criticism: that no profitable exchange can take place without agreement over basic premises. The rain that day was not unusual in Melbourne but as we knew from our arrival there, the weather could also turn very hot. One memory I have is of my wife with her feet in a bucket of cold water as she typed up my Ph.D. thesis under our sweltering, corrugated-iron roof. Being in Australia was a good excuse for not submitting this thesis, but at the end of three years I was due six months' leave from my university and I had decided that, before the patience of the Cambridge authorities ran out and they refused to grant me any more extensions, I would go back to England then and try my luck. The other writing I must have worked on at this time was an essay called 'The Irony of *Mansfield Park*', which eventually appeared in *The Melbourne Critical Review*. This was a largely unconscious declaration of Leavisian affiliation in that *Mansfield Park* as Jane Austen's best, most complex novel had been an article of Downing faith, and *The Melbourne Critical Review*, closely associated with Goldberg, was probably at that time the most Leavisian of all the world's literary journals (*The Cambridge Quarterly* having declined to compete for that title).

A further occasion on which I displayed my Leavisian colours came when I was asked by my professor to respond to a request for a talk on *Othello* which he had received from a literary society in Bendigo. This is a town a long way inland from Melbourne and, like Ballarat, a consequence of the State of Victoria's gold rush in the mid-nineteenth century. As everyone knows, the vast majority of Australians live around the edges of their continent, in highly populated coastal cities. For some of the same reasons that made me so fond of George Eliot, I liked the towns of inland Victoria which always seemed to me to have a quite special feel, as of people bravely flying the flag or boldly asserting themselves in an environment made to seem old-fashioned by an inability or disinclination to replace fine old buildings as rapidly as they were replaced in the city. I can remember travelling in a car through mile upon mile of desert-like bush and suddenly passing through a tiny settlement where women in all-white dresses and hats were playing bowls. It reminded me of a story Merimée tells of Stendhal and the retreat from Russia. An officer in Napoleon's Grand Army, Stendhal's ability to appear clean-shaven and well-dressed every morning, in spite of all the horrendous material difficulties, so impressed one of his superiors that he told him '*vous êtes un homme de coeur*'. But this, I now see, was not only an extravagant comparison but a patronising one. The ladies on the bowling green were no doubt perfectly happy and at ease in their environment, as why should they not have been? The same goes for those I met at the Bendigo literary society, even if it was one of them who, after my talk on *Othello* was over, asked if I had any news of 'the home country'.

I did not feel that I had much of my own to say about *Othello* and therefore fell back on an essay on the play which Leavis had first published in *Scrutiny* and then in *The Common Pursuit*: 'Diabolic intellect and the noble hero: or The Sentimentalist's Othello'. This was one of only three studies of Shakespeare's plays he wrote, the other two being on *Measure for Measure* and the last plays; yet the verse of Shakespeare was crucial to his thinking. In the chapter of *Education and the University* entitled 'Literary Studies', he uses a soliloquy from *Macbeth* to demonstrate how inadequate our usual ideas of metaphor and simile are; and he would often refer back to what he called a 'critical exercise' – the comparison between Dryden's version of *Antony and Cleopatra* and Shakespeare's original which he had published in *Scrutiny* in 1936. The importance of this last piece was not only that it showed the difference between verse which 'enacts' its meaning and merely states it. What the comparison also illustrated for him was that radical change in English which had occurred in the seventeenth century and which he related to equally radical changes in the nation's economic and cultural life. Shakespeare's language was the touchstone for Leavis, as it has been for so many other critics. That he never wrote much on the plays was therefore a matter for self-reproach, as those of us to whom he talked about tragedy were made to feel (it was not so much tragedy in general about which he felt he still had things to say but *Hamlet* and *King Lear*). Newton's article on *Scrutiny*'s failure with Shakespeare may therefore have hit a raw nerve. Its ostensible targets were L. C. Knights and D. A. Traversi, who were the journal's chief contributors as far as Shakespeare was concerned; but Leavis was criticised for having endorsed their work and implicitly so for having failed to provide more material himself. If this last charge proved especially galling, it would have been because Leavis had already made it against himself.

My lecture in Bendigo was not entirely a repetition of what Leavis had had to say. His claim was that when one looks carefully at the way Othello speaks, it is clear that he is made vulnerable to Iago's insinuations not so much by his colour, age and unfamiliarity with Venetian social life but above all by an egotism which expresses itself in self-dramatisations of a self-approving kind. There is an ignorance of his own nature which lasts right up until his suicide and is particularly evident in his claim to be 'not easily jealous', so that the dawning self-understanding characteristic of the conclusion of many tragedies never occurs. The sentimentalists who idealised him (A. C. Bradley was the critic Leavis had principally in mind) could only explain Othello's downfall by exaggerating the cunning and intelligence of Iago when he was really 'not much more than a dramatic mechanism'. What I tried to argue was that this was an exaggeration and I produced different examples from those of Leavis in order to illustrate an argument that was nevertheless essentially his. That is to say that the whole drift of my lecture was anti-Bradleyian so that, in developing my case, I found myself also discussing Leavis's alternative notion – not so evident in the *Othello* essay as elsewhere – of a Shakespeare play as a dramatic poem. This was the orthodoxy, much more dependent on reading than seeing, with which *Scrutiny* attempted to loosen Bradley's grip in the schools. Newton's complaint was that it had been too successful and that, in its move away from endless discussion of the characters in a Shakespeare play as if they lived next door, it had encouraged a bloodless search through details of the language for dominating themes. He contrasted various general statements about Shakespeare by Knights and Traversi with passages from Bradley which, in spite of his supposed methodological naïveté (and was he not in any event aware that the number of Lady Macbeth's possible children was a trivial matter?), demonstrated a much more sensitive and humane engagement with the plays. My listeners in Bendigo were almost certainly brought up on Bradley. I still feel that the case Leavis made against his approach to *Othello* was right if unnecessarily abusive – he referred to Bradley's 'comical solemnity', said he was 'completely wrong-headed', and described his reading as 'grossly and palpably false' to the evidence the play offered. But I also still feel uneasy about being the bearer of recent critical news from the city to the middle class, middle aged ladies who mostly made up my audience in Bendigo, and remain in two minds about the appropriateness of having suggested they replace the unalloyed pity they may have previously felt for Othello with more mixed and complicated feelings.

Six months' leave after only three years at La Trobe struck me as extremely generous. When we flew out of Australia at the end of 1970 we left behind most of our possessions because we fully expected to return there. The cheapest flight was to Frankfurt from where we drove to Annecy, the picture-postcard town, only thirty or so miles from Geneva and the Swiss border, which is where my wife's parents happened to live. My thesis had previously been posted off to Cambridge so that I now had to find something to do. The leave I had been granted was after all officially designated as *study* leave and although it was still possible at this period to use the free time for the preparation of more teaching (a new course, for example), there was a growing expectation that it should result in a publication of some nature. Not having anything particular in mind, I went back to Stendhal. I had been impressed by reading the 'composite' biography of D. H. Lawrence, put together by an American scholar called Edward Nehls. He had collected numerous impressions of Lawrence from family members, close friends, bitter enemies and casual contacts and arranged them around a spare biographical framework. The result made an ideal life-story and I began collecting material in the hope of eventually being able to do something similar for Stendhal. Meanwhile I thought I might try my hand at translating. The autobiographical writings were what chiefly interested me but my favourite among them, the *Vie de Henry Brulard*, had been translated into English many times. I therefore settled on the much more obscure *Souvenirs d'Égotisme* and with the help of my wife, as well as some of her relatives, began trying to render Stendhal's loose, racy idiom into English.

When I eventually finished *Memoirs of an Egotist*, as I decided to call Stendhal's short text, I had quite literally no idea whether it was publishable and, if it was, who might bring it out. I remembered having seen roughly similar texts bearing the imprint of the Hogarth Press and posted several chapters and an introduction off there. I did not know that Hogarth had long been taken over by Chatto and Windus, and that my enclosures would therefore pass across Dennis Enright's desk. He liked what he saw and persuaded his firm to publish the book. Thanks to a flattering lead review from John Bayley in *The Spectator*, it had a modest success. Enright told me that Sylvia Townsend Warner, who was a Chatto author, had asked to read the book and described it afterwards as a *succès d'estime*. What she probably meant to confirm was that very few copies had been sold. If I nevertheless look back on it with pleasure, it is partly because (in contrast to my later experience) the whole business of seeing the book through the press had proved so painless; but chiefly that translation has always struck me as such a relatively *innocent* activity. Translators are of course the helots of the literary scene. Those who translate professionally are notoriously underpaid and anyone who relied on translating for academic advancement would be seriously deranged. Their work can only be properly estimated by someone who knows the text and the two languages as well or better than they do and can therefore judge the myriad of choices that have to be made in rendering one language into another. The result is that translations are not really reviewable. All reviewers can usually do (apart from having their say on the author translated) is decide whether or not the text 'reads well' and concentrate on the introduction, which is how John Bayley dealt with me, fortunately. But the rich rewards of translating are first of all co-habitation over a long period with an author you love (perhaps the same could be said of editing), and then the sense that you might possibly be doing some good. This is important at a stage of life when it becomes critical to be able to say that at least you never did too much harm.

We could not stay with my wife's parents for ever and I knew that I would soon be called for my Ph.D. viva in Cambridge. It was a question of finding somewhere to live in England where I had access to a university library. We choose Canterbury because a fellow student and close friend of mine from Downing had found a job at the university there, as had my former supervisor Morris Shapira. It was through them that I got to know other members of the Kent English department. In Cambridge, Shapira had known well two of Goldberg's closest colleagues who had moved with him from Melbourne to Sydney and then, after the departmental split, back again. That may have had something to do with his feeling that he would like to spend a year in Australia and an arrangement was made whereby he would replace me at La Trobe while I filled in for him at Kent. Towards the end of this exchange year Kent found that they had more English posts to fill and I was asked if I would like to stay on permanently. With many regrets about leaving Australia, I said yes and, after much friendly bending of La Trobe's rules about study leave from Derick Marsh, became a permanent rather than a temporary member of the English department at the University of Kent.

With colleagues I found congenial and children in school, I remained at Kent for the rest of my career. I had two years on exchange in first Massachusetts and then Indiana, and another year at the wondrous National Center for the Humanities in North Carolina, together with one or two study leave excursions; but in general I stayed put. Reproaching myself one day for not having made more effort to move, I came across in *Scrutiny* some striking thoughts on travel by James Smith. I said earlier that the bulk of the commentary on Shakespeare in that journal came from L. C. Knights and D. A. Traversi, and that is true; but Smith contributed pieces on *As You Like It* and *Much Ado About Nothing*. In the first of these he considers Jaques's world-weariness, or what he more philosophically thinks of as his 'scepticism', and evaluates his claim to have benefitted from having been that familiar target of Elizabethan and Jacobean satire, 'a traveller':

> The travels to which Jaques refers the origin of his scepticism are equally likely to have been its consequence, for travel and exploration degenerate into habit. When the senses are dazzled by a ceaseless and rapid change of objects, the intellect has no time to discriminate between them, the will no occasion for choice, so that in the end a man becomes capable of neither. The habit is then a necessity of life, which at the same time and to the same extent has slackened, become languid. It concerns itself only with the surface of objects while their substance is neglected.

This is highly distinctive writing and at the same time (to my mind) slightly peculiar in tone, given the kind of play and character being discussed. On the several occasions Leavis reflected on the achievement of *Scrutiny*, he would tend to mention Smith as one of its most distinguished contributors and declare himself particularly proud of having published, in a very early number, an essay by him on Metaphysical Poetry. That he appreciated a style of thinking so different from his own illustrates the variety of *Scrutiny* and is another argument against the common charge that he was narrow-minded.

Smith is relevant to the one serious attempt I did make to move away from Kent, not long after I had become a permanent staff member. A post was advertised at the University of Fribourg in Switzerland and I sent in my application. I was familiar with Lausanne from my visit there to see Jean-Marc Berthoud and I had often travelled in my father-in-law's car to and from Geneva. He used to fill up with petrol in Switzerland because it was cheaper there than in France and smuggle back home Swiss equipment for his dental surgery. Deceiving the border customs was a local French pastime and I used to be dumb-founded by the assurance with which he would say, when asked if he had anything to declare, '*Absolument rien, monsieur*'. Some of that assurance I needed when I was invited to Fribourg to give a lecture, but it seemed to go well enough. The town itself was a disappointment after the other two in Switzerland I knew and it was disconcerting that most people in it seemed to speak Swiss German – officially bi-lingual, Fribourg is on a linguistic border. But that could only be a challenge and everything was progressing well when the Dean of Humanities took me aside to discuss a few administrative matters. 'There is one thing I need to ask you', he said suavely, 'Are you a Catholic?' When I confessed that I wasn't he looked a little disappointed but then added that it did not matter very much because there were already several members of the *Église Reformée* on the teaching staff. There was nothing that was unsophisticated about the Dean but he gave me a foretaste of the form I saw in Indiana which contained a section on religion without a box for 'None' (or even, if I recall correctly, 'Other'). I cannot remember whether, when we returned home, I politely rejected a job offer that was made to me or withdrew my application. Either way I saved myself some difficulty, and rather more than I understood at the time. It was only later I realised that, after working for the British Council in Venezuela, James Smith had eventually wound up at the University of Fribourg. In the essay on the Metaphysicals Leavis admired, Smith argues that the way Donne deploys metaphysics has more in common with Thomas Aquinas than Dante or Lucretius and in the process displays a knowledge of Aquinas that suggests he was a Catholic. I learnt later from Enright (who had been supervised by Smith at Downing) that he was in fact a Catholic convert and that Fribourg was a natural place for him to go because, in ways I had not appreciated when I was there, it was a famous centre of Catholic theology. In a biographical note on him appended to a collection of his writings, he is described as having lived in Fribourg in 'a religious house'. He was clearly an immensely knowledgeable man, polyglot and polymathic. His references to Aquinas, Dante and Lucretius in his essay on Metaphysical Poetry are bolstered with others to Virgil, Tasso and Calderón; and his later contributions to *Scrutiny* included pieces on Croce, Baudelaire and Mallarmé as well as Chapman, Wordsworth and Alfred North Whitehead. In so far, therefore, as I might have been regarded as a replacement from the same stable, I saved my putative employers from being grievously disappointed, and myself the embarrassment of explaining why even *Église Reformée* would not cover my case.

SIXTEEN

TEACHING IN THE UK

The senior members of the English staff at Kent were not unsympathetic to Leavisian principles. The most senior among them (a well-known Shakespearian) could be irritated when I joined with the close friend I mentioned to propose the inclusion or exclusion of texts from certain courses, or expressed scepticism about a degree in film studies he was anxious to establish. When I turned up for a committee one day and someone pointed out that it was not my name but my friend's which was on the list of appointed members, he muttered grumpily under his breath, 'Same thing'. After his return from Australia, and before a premature and tragic death, Morris Shapira could also be a thorn in his flesh. But he was fundamentally fair-minded and, in the moments when he objected to the three of us, it was less because we had all been to Downing than that we were all from Cambridge. A Birmingham graduate, he resented the dominance of Oxford and Cambridge in the English system and rightly felt that those universities too often exerted an authority they did not deserve, and had not earned.

Kent was a new university (so that I have never worked permanently in any other kind), and the atmosphere in its early days was egalitarian, friendly and optimistic. The chief innovation of the Humanities Faculty was that students in their first four terms all had to take a majority of courses which were interdisciplinary. Under titles such as 'Contemporary Society and its Background', 'Science and Religion' or 'Colonialism and the Emergent Nations', English would find itself combined with History, one of the foreign languages, Philosophy, Theology or even (in a daring 'cross-Faculty' move)

Sociology. Leavis had always recognised the importance of what he came to refer to as disciplines 'allied' to his own, and felt that the study of English literature naturally led out towards other areas of interest. But in his scheme, which was consistent with his belief in his subject as the core of any humane education, the preliminary to engagement with these other disciplines was concentration for two years on English itself. Kent turned this model on its head for reasons which had a lot to do with early specialisation in the schools. Pupils at 15 or 16 who were not studying maths or science, and wanted to move on to A level, had in those days a relatively narrow choice in front of them, while certain university subjects, philosophy being the chief example, were not taught in schools at all. The first four terms at Kent gave undergraduates an opportunity to look around and decide what they might really want to study. In such a liberal regime, the Leavisian notion of English as somehow central was bound to disappear, although there was one way in which it did retain that status, *primus inter pares*. It was a very popular subject with hordes of applicants so that one of the effects of the interdisciplinary structure was to distribute students more evenly, moving some of those who had come up intending to study English on to areas likely to be under-populated.

For the staff involved, the interdisciplinary Part One at Kent could be an enlightening experience. With what would be now seen as the luxury of 'tandem teaching', it introduced them to methodologies and attitudes different from their own and drove them to reappraise what they believed. Whether or not it brought equivalent benefits to the students, it soon came under pressures which would destroy it. One was that it did not always, or perhaps often, fit in well with a particular teacher's current research. This began to matter more as research increased in importance and many new members of staff, expected to publish early, found themselves obliged to plough a narrow furrow and concentrate on their specialisms rather than range more freely. There was in any case a natural tendency for subjects to retreat back into their own domains, Leavis not being the only person to believe that his or her discipline was more important than any other. As time went on, having one's own students assumed an importance which was more than intellectual so that perhaps the single greatest pressure came from those famous unintended consequences of an apparently simple administrative measure, the move towards devolved budgets. When every subject has to work out how much it spends and set that against the amount each student it teaches is worth, the inclination to hand over any of your 'own' students to others is likely to decrease. The introduction of fees came very late but it was only perhaps a natural culmination of a tendency to visualise undergraduates as individuals with set sums of money inscribed on their foreheads. Why would one want to give such valuable property away?

I never heard Leavis explicitly defend English as the most important of the subjects in the Humanities, but he often, in his writings, assumed that to be the case. I have already suggested that part of the argument, in so far as it had any development, was that English was concerned with the native language without which anything we call culture could not exist. The linguistic achievements of the past were embodied in great literary works which it needed alert critics to recognise and interpret. A university should therefore be a centre for the particular kind of non-specialised intelligence which a training in English should ideally provide. The more people had this, the more society would be protected, not only against the lowering of standards in the literary periodicals and other media, but also in the nation's cultural life as a whole. Quite recently, the BBC produced a three part television series on *Great Thinkers of the 20th century*. The chief criterion for inclusion seems to have been the BBC's possession of archive material so that when, in the third part, Leavis appeared, it was because a lecture he gave at the Cheltenham Literary Festival in 1968 happened to have been recorded (in general he was highly resistant to having any contacts with the BBC and this was therefore the only sound archive available). The short extract from the lecture chosen to represent him, and to accompany a few still photographic portraits, or footage of various parts of Cambridge, seemed to me unfortunate. In a public voice that sounded more high pitched and prissy that any I was used to, he was heard to ask what the state of the 'industrial masses' must be when 'they save their living for their leisure but don't know how to use it except in the bingo hall, filling pools' forms, spending money, eating fish and chips in Spain. Nothing but emptiness that has to be filled with drink, sex, eating, background music and what the papers and the telly supply'. This brief passage was prefaced by a young talking head who, with exemplary political correctness, warned viewers that they were about to hear 'an outrageous rant against the working classes' and who, when the passage was over, characterised it as a 'shockingly elitist outburst'.

The context of Leavis's talk makes clear his genuine concern for the way those whose forbears had laboured away in dark satanic mills had been exploited by modern industrial society and denied their cultural heritage. But when he refers to 'industrial masses' he is using a very broad term. Not all of those who work in the modern industrial system have jobs which are mind-numbing and the variety of ways in which they spend their leisure time is considerable, much more so than Leavis (who did not get out much) suggests. Why, moreover, he thought that drink, sex and eating involved necessarily reprehensible activities is not clear. In his view, everybody has what he called a 'hunger for significance' without which no satisfactory life is possible, the need for some ulterior spiritual aim. Be that as if may, it is surprising how many people can manage quite well by confining themselves to short-term objectives, involved as they are with how their children are progressing at school, when they will next see their friends, the possibility of a pay rise at work. All the many different ways in which such people spend their spare time would no doubt have been classified by Pascal as *divertissements* but then, if his own theological solution to the emptiness of life is ruled out, the only response to his grim picture of our existence has to be a valorisation of the various projects, activities and enjoyments which constitute our here and now, however lacking in ultimate meaning they might appear to be. In pre-capitalist times, and for a good while afterwards, spiritual significance was given to the mass of the people by the Church; but that this was an altogether good thing is, at the very least, debatable. In stigmatising modern working-class pastimes, Leavis was implicitly suggesting that there were periods when they were more wholesome and less offensive to the taste of someone brought up as he was. Whether or not this is so, the real problem for the Leavisite was to know how a training in literary criticism was going to affect the situation one way or the other for, if its social impact was to be minimal (or non-existent), then the usefulness of English was called in question and its claim to be the key subject in a Faculty of Humanities badly damaged.

One could be sceptical about any broad social mission English might have and still believe that it was a subject well worth teaching in a Leavisian fashion. There were, however, various factors which made that belief increasingly difficult to hang on to. Chief among these was the question of numbers, that very university expansion to which I owed my job (at least the paradox did not escape me). I can remember fierce arguments as to whether the number of students in a supervision could be increased from four to six, and then from six to eight. The final solution meant seminars of sixteen and made any teaching along Leavisian lines difficult to maintain. Many Oxbridge colleagues supported the change because their memory of supervisions was of reading out their essays to a somnolent don whereas at Downing our work had always been read beforehand. They also felt that seeing a number of couples or quartets of students in succession led to teachers often having to repeat themselves. Perhaps it did but my own sense of the difficulty of small group teaching along Leavisian lines was that, to be successful, it required me to have read, or more likely, to have re-read, the text under discussion quite recently. By flicking through it the night before, I could refresh my memory as to feelings and conclusions previously experienced or arrived at, but this was not the same as sharing with the students the results of a fresh encounter. Yet to be always in the position of having just re-read what they had been reading was hard, and often impossible.

Matters were not made any simpler by the preliminary training many students were then receiving from the schools. More and more, the texts they had studied before coming to university may have included a Shakespeare play, or a selection from the Romantic poets, but were predominantly from the twentieth century. This meant that most of what is thought of as English literature was difficult for them to read. They may have chosen English over French or German at A level because the latter were associated with a set amount of hard grind and learning by rote; but no-one can read Swift's *Tale of a Tub*, or a late novel by James, without recognising that English is also a linguistic discipline. There are in both semantic and perhaps above all syntactical challenges which they quite naturally found very difficult and to which the most obvious answer was habituation. The sensible move would therefore have been to study fewer texts at a slower rate but there were pressures against that procedure from many quarters, and not least from the students themselves. For many different parties, courses needed to at least *look* sophisticated (even in those days marketing was beginning to be important), and secondary reading lists for English courses habitually appeared that would have tested the capacities of speed readers with IQs which qualified them for MENSA. The disparity between those lists and primary texts the students could not read with any ease sometimes produced a strange phenomenon. With the help of the reading lists and the lectures, there were those who could talk impressively about certain works, many moments in which it turned out they could not understand. As practical criticism exercises faded away, there was no mechanism for checking how often this happened although the issue was not in any case a matter of critical appreciation but of meaning in the most straightforward sense. The cases to which I am referring were no doubt rare: gifted students fared as they always do, the less gifted battled bravely on, and those who fell by the wayside often did so happily, or even deliberately. But that such a category could exist at all was worrying in that it indicated not merely a failure to do good but the commission of possible harm, even if the ability to talk fluently about a matter you do not fully understand is perhaps as marketable a skill as any other.

The combination of institutional and social change left the Leavisite standing on ground which was continually eroded: like someone on a desert island slowly being engulfed by the sea. The sensible move would have been to abandon the territory altogether but if literary criticism is not at the centre of English as a university discipline, I used to ask myself, what is? Inculcating a more liberal attitude to other ethnic groups, women and social issues in general through English literature gave some a strong rationale for teaching it; and there must have been others for whom literary scholarship was a sufficient end in itself and who therefore conveyed that message to the students. In spite of an argument in this second case about the acquisition of skills and intellectual discipline similar to the one that had been used in the past to defend compulsory Latin, I found it difficult to see the point of a training in literary scholarship for young people who were in the main not going to become academics. For a brief moment, and in a few places, the Leavisian ideal had enjoyed a dominance which had given coherence to English teaching at university level; but in the 1970s there was little hope of consensus and the subject was becoming fissiparous. From it at Kent grew degrees in both film and drama, and then in media studies, while its inborn tendency to mutate into cultural history was enormously strengthened by the impact of 'theory' in all its various forms. In these circumstances, to continue to feel that encouraging students to read what were often complex texts in an alert and critical manner was in and of itself a useful activity, you had to believe that there was an effect of doing so which was beneficial, if not to society as a whole then at least to the individual.

Arguments of very different kinds were mounted against this last view. Critics as different as George Steiner and Terry Eagleton pointed out that some of those in charge of the Nazi concentration camps had been cultivated men who listened to Mozart and read Goethe; while, on a quite different level, it was sometimes observed that Leavis's inwardness with the great works of English literature did not result in any noticeable sweetness and light in his own personal relations (a point made by David Hare in the segment on Leavis in the *Great Thinkers of the 20th century* programme). But the case for the beneficial effects of reading great literature is not destroyed by a counter example and much more would need to be said about this or that Nazi camp commandant in order to be sure that he constituted a decisive one. As for Leavis, it is possible that the situations he found himself in sometimes required something other than sweetness and light. No sensible person has in any case ever thought that there was some direct and automatic route between a sensitive appreciation of a work of art and exemplary behaviour, but that Shakespeare, Pope, Wordsworth, Dickens and a host of others offer their readers the possibility of a greater understanding of both their social and natural environment, as well as of themselves, seems a reasonable article of faith. So too does the idea that these writers introduce their readers to feelings, attitudes and thoughts which they would not otherwise have known. Whether the results of this enlarged experience make its beneficiaries better citizens would be impossible to demonstrate, but it was difficult to go on teaching English without some lurking suspicion that it did.

As admirers of Leavis became more isolated, they were brought closer to those who defended the traditional canon in a spirit similar to the one at work in the society for the preservation of old buildings. But the past was for him always recreated by the present and in the 1920s and '30s it had been re-formed for him by Eliot, and then Lawrence. He was particularly fond of the dictum of Eliot's which is hidden away in an introduction he wrote to a selection of Dr Johnson's poetry and which says that, although sensibility may change from generation to generation, expression is only altered by a man of genius. This supported what seems to have been a natural inclination in him to associate truly revolutionary literary work with technical innovation. The proof was to be found in Eliot's own writing but there was a problem in so far as Joyce and Woolf were both far more glaringly innovative than Lawrence. Yet, as Leavis showed in *D. H. Lawrence: Novelist*, it was possible to make out a case for *The Rainbow* and *Women in Love* as groundbreaking in their methods. The most obvious truth about Lawrence and Eliot however, is that they were both driven by what they saw in their society to take on major themes. Among many other distinguishing characteristics of Lawrence's two novels, for example, is an attempt to describe the effect on individuals of England's change from an agricultural to an industrial society; and after the First World War, Eliot's concern in his poetry with life in a world without religious faith becomes very obvious. It was not easy to find in their successors writers who possessed either the will or the ability to be similarly ambitious. Beckett might surprise one with the variety and humour with which he could express an essentially nihilistic view of the world, and Larkin proved that it was still possible to write excellent poetry about ordinary matters and in ordinary language, using traditional verse forms. But neither of these, nor a dozen others who were becoming established minor classics in the 1970s, made an impact similar to Eliot's or provided a stimulus at all like the one which had provoked Leavis's 'revaluation' of the past. In the debris of a post-war world it had clearly been exciting for him to reconfigure the history of English literature, to take 'new bearings'. Forty or fifty years later, the Leavisite who looked round for a base from which to launch the most modest personal version of that enterprise, was likely to be disappointed. It may be that his training prevented him from looking in the right places or, more probably, that the increased variety and fragmentation of the cultural world – the accelerated pace at which any homogeneity it may once have had was breaking up – made the search senseless.

SEVENTEEN

LAWRENCE

A perhaps more significant illustration of the unintended consequences of social action than devolved budgets was the government's introduction of the 'research assessment exercise', the infamous RAE (as it used to be called). The attitude to research when I first began teaching was relaxed. One of our external examiners at Kent once described to us how, at a set time every year, the senior English professor at his own university would stalk down the departmental corridor, knocking on every door. If members of his staff talked of the new courses in which they had been involved, he would tell them they ought to think about publishing more; if they described what they had just written, he would warn them against neglecting their pedagogic responsibilities. One of the reasons we found this comic was because there was so little pressure on us to write. People would publish, it was assumed, when they felt they had something to say and, for some of us, 'research' was in any case hardly the most felicitous term to describe what came before saying that something. But in its grants to universities the government allocated certain set sums for research and it was decided it should try to discover whether it was getting its money's worth. Finding out how much each department had published, and devising an inevitably inadequate method for judging its quality, meant that there was a handy criterion available for comparing one university with another; but the most obvious, unintended effect of the new system was the down-grading of teaching, especially when the grants any university received began to be affected by its showing in the RAE. Then it was that teaching came to be regarded as something most people were able to manage competently *anyway*, and the only method of distinguishing between individuals, or departments, became the number of articles and books published. The difference this made was profound. At Kent, the contact hours each staff member had with students had crept up to twelve (a derisorily low number for a school teacher, but considered quite high in the university world). After the RAE had been in operation for some time, it was decided that, by increasing class sizes, twelve hours could be reduced to six so that staff members would have more time for their own work. The university therefore became more like those we had heard of in the States where 'publish or perish' was the mantra; but also more like those on the continent – the ones I had wanted to work in – where the classes were large and their teachers infrequent visitors. The radical change in attitudes had many different aspects but it was epitomised for me when we lost a young, much published professor and the vice-chancellor told our head of department to find himself 'another star'.

Had I ever been conscious of a professional need to write, I would have realised that it posed a special problem for Leavisites, much like the one I encountered in having to give a lecture. Since there seemed no point in conveying to students information available in books, what could a lecture be other than an example of critical practice? An article or book could similarly only offer a critical reading, a contribution to debate about this or that text. In the 1970s and '80s such readings were still being published, but the market for them was declining rapidly. Following my translation of Stendhal, I continued to explore the many different strategies of autobiographical writing. I came to Wordsworth because he was my favourite poet. I thought 'The Ruined Cottage', 'Michael' and many of the shorter poems were masterpieces, and I was entirely convinced by the idea that he was one of those geniuses who, in Eliot's words, altered expression. The Prelude fascinated me, especially in its first two books, but I was puzzled by the fact that although certain crucial episodes from his childhood which Wordsworth remembered, the so-called 'spots of time', were largely terrifying and traumatic, he could nevertheless regard them as sources of future strength. I set out from this paradox to offer an interpretation of the poem, sceptically evaluating the relevance of Freud along the way. This was hermeneutics rather than critical reading in the Leavisian sense, but at least I felt I was addressing a genuine problem that needed a solution. My qualifications for providing it were challenged by a friend who, apart from suggesting that a suitable title for the book which was emerging from my enquiries would be The Visionary Dreariness (a phrase from one of the more striking spots of time), pointed out that whenever I was with him in the Kent countryside I could hardly tell one flower from another. This was quite true and I had no illusions about ever being properly equipped to become a worshipper of Nature in Wordsworth's sense of that term; but it seemed to me that he was a great psychological poet and that it was legitimate to consider him largely in that light.

Where I would have gone after Wordsworth, I have no idea and there did not appear at the time any particular urgency to find one. My life was changed by friendship with yet another South African exile with a hatred of apartheid. Mark Kinkead-Weekes had escaped to Oxford on a Rhodes scholarship and, when I first knew him, was principally an eighteenth-century specialist, busy completing a huge book on Richardson. But he had also written a widely admired article on the slow emergence of Lawrence's *The Rainbow* and *Women in Love* from a novel in draft initially entitled *The Sisters*. The textual history of this process, including as it did transition via Lawrence's often baffling long essay, the *Study of Thomas Hardy*, was unusually complicated; but he had explicated it with extraordinary care and precision, revealing in the process a strong affinity with those aspects of Lawrence's nature that might be described as religious or even, on occasions, mystical. It may have been this work which helped to persuade Cambridge University Press that he would be the right person to write a new biography of Lawrence, as a companion piece to their new edition of his works and letters. But these last two enterprises were throwing up huge mounds of new material, enough to make Kinkead-Weekes feel that he would need collaborators if there were to be any chance of completing the project in reasonable time. He himself very naturally wanted to deal with the crucial war years, when the two great novels whose origins he had already explored were written. For the early period, there was an ideal candidate at hand in John Worthen, who had been an undergraduate at Downing only a few years after me, when Leavis was no longer director of studies but still teaching there; and who had then come to Kent in order to write a thesis on the reception of Lawrence's earlier novels. The last years, from the time Lawrence left Europe for America in 1922 until his death in 1930, must have seemed trickier. If I was asked to make up the trio, it may have been because it was known I was interested in life-writing (and from the outside, there must have seemed little difference between an interest in autobiography and biography). Subscribing to the common view that there is no better introduction to Lawrence than his travel book *Sea and Sardinia*, I had also written a short article on this text in which I had tried to analyse how it managed to convey such a remarkable impression of immediacy. Yet apart from the fact that Mark Kinkead-Weekes and I got on well (a necessary condition for collaboration), it may have been that an additional reason for my being approached was that I had been at Downing. By this period Leavis was inextricably associated with Lawrence in the public mind. Even while I was still at Cambridge, I once heard someone childishly intoning, 'Who is DHL? Like FRL, only he wrote novels.'

The offer Mark Kinkead-Weekes made to me, I almost immediately accepted, without much thought. It seemed an interesting project and, besides, with two volumes of the biography to appear before mine was due, the moment of delivery was a long way off. I was vaguely conscious that because Lawrence's reputation among academics had peaked in the 1960s and been in steady decline since, I was joining a sinking ship; but that did not bother me. I was more concerned by the semi-jocular abuse I received from D. J. Enright when he heard what I was up to. From his position within publishing, Enright had been able to observe the rapid rise in the popularity of biography, one manifestation of which had been the award of a contract rumoured to be worth over half a million to Michael Holroyd, following the success of his life of Lytton Strachey. Enright was not mollified when I told him that my own advance from CUP was £200 since, apart from his conviction that the success of the Strachey life, or of that of Proust by George Painter, was too much associated with both subjects' sex lives, his real complaint was that the public was being increasingly encouraged to read *about* authors rather than anything by them. There was justification in this charge, but at least I could claim that there was nothing in writing a biography of Lawrence which was clearly against Leavisian principles. It was common in this period to associate Leavis and his admirers with the so-called 'New Critics' in America because both parties were insistent on paying close attention to verbal texture. But they took a doctrinaire stance on the relation of biographical information to literary analysis, claiming it had no role to play at all, whereas Leavis was always linking the work to its author, bringing in biographical details whenever it suited him. In his chapter on Wordsworth in *Revaluation*, after quoting from 'The Ruined Cottage' the lines, 'In my despite / I thought of that poor Woman as of one / Whom I had known and loved', he comments: 'No doubt the particular memory of Annette asserts itself here'; and examples of this kind are ubiquitous in his work. His review of Aldous Huxley's collection of Lawrence's letters, which appeared in the first volume of *Scrutiny*, begins, 'There are some writers a serious interest in whose work leads inevitably to a discussion of their personalities'; and towards the start of *D. H. Lawrence: Novelist* he writes, 'But it is impossible to study the work and art [of Lawrence] without forming a vivid sense of the man, and touching on the facts of his history'.

For three people to be writing the biography of one man was unusual, and perhaps a little strange. Sometimes I used to think of that children's game in which one player draws a head, folds back the paper so that it cannot be seen and leaves a second player to attach a torso. The same procedure is followed when the third player draws the legs so that, as the paper is finally unfolded, a figure often emerges which is comically grotesque. We tried to avoid this effect by meeting regularly and scrutinising carefully each other's work although, because we were three very different people, different emphases inevitably appeared. So much the better, we argued, especially when dealing with such a volatile and many-faceted individual as Lawrence. As the work progressed, I began to see that there were disadvantages in being responsible for volume 3. Perhaps the most important of them was that an agenda had already been set by the time I came to write. It was by then already informally established, for instance, that everything Lawrence wrote should receive a mention, not such a tall order early on or in mid-career, but in my period there was a vast number of small pieces or poems, which perhaps helps to explain why, although in my volume I dealt with only eight years of his life, it turned out to be well over 700 pages long (a door-stop is how *Private Eye* described it). I used to tease John Worthen by saying that although I could apply for grants to visit New Mexico, he could only ask for the bus fare to Nottingham; but there is no doubt that the early life – childhood and background – is often the most interesting part of any biography. Mark Kinkead-Weekes held the advantage of having at the centre of his work the two most important and ambitious novels Lawrence ever wrote. After *Women in Love*, none of the novels is of the same quality and I came to feel, with regard to the sinking ship of Lawrence's reputation, that nothing would change unless both *The Plumed Serpent* and *Lady Chatterley's Lover* could somehow be pitched overboard. Making my way through their various versions, I occasionally felt like Proust's Swann who, after his affair with Odette is over, begins to wonder how he could have spent so much time on someone who was fundamentally not his type. And yet falling into my period, in addition to those two novels, were some remarkable tales, *The Princess* and *St. Mawr* but above all *The Virgin and the Gypsy*, and very many excellent short stories. There was also an abundance of important literary criticism, in essays or reviews, including *Studies in Classic American Literature*, as well as much discursive writing of great interest. In addition to *Mornings in Mexico* (which I enjoyed more than *The Plumed Serpent*), there was the moving *Etruscan Places* and some of the poems Lawrence wrote towards the end of his life are very fine indeed. Taken together, these works would by themselves have justified Lawrence's claim to be one of the greatest writers of the twentieth century so that I never regretted my bargain, especially since I had available what neither of my collaborators enjoyed, a natural conclusion.

There was nothing in Leavis's writing which positively precluded biographical study (although he detested the thought of it ever being focussed on himself), but that does not mean I believed he would have approved of what I was doing. In fact, I was sure he would not. This had nothing to do with *The Plumed Serpent* or *Lady Chatterley's Lover*, neither of which he thought much of. Leavis struggled hard with the claim Lawrence made in the relief of having finally finished the first of these novels that it was the most important thing he had done so far; but he could never bring himself to believe that long stretches of *The Plumed Serpent* were anything but boring. In a preliminary attempt to come to terms with Lawrence in 1932, he had praised *Lady Chatterley* for its artistic maturity; but that was at a time when he thought both *The Rainbow* and *Women in Love* hard to get through and what seemed to impress him most in the later novel was its attack on industrialism. As his thinking about Lawrence developed, *Lady Chatterley* slid lower and lower down his scale of values, and there was in any event always a disinclination in him to engage fully with Lawrence's interest in sex. Leavis would not therefore (I believe) have disapproved of the attempt in my volume of the biography to push these two novels a little to one side; but the idea of Lawrence which emerges from his *D. H. Lawrence: Novelist* is very different from what my own became. This book was often criticised, if not mocked, for its over-use of superlatives: superb, supreme, unsurpassable, incomparable, astonishing, marvellous, wonderful all appear regularly, together with generous sprinklings of the word genius. It was also felt that it relied far too heavily on quotations, some of them very long. Both of these features, it seemed to me, could be associated with frustration. How could anyone with even a modicum of literary intelligence read through its extensive quotations from Lawrence's description of Tom Brangwen about to go courting, for example, and not recognise immediately that here was novel-writing as accomplished and original as any in the century? And how could people not see, from the very varied examples of his prose Leavis provided, that there was no other English writer of the time whose range was so impressive?

If these were indeed the questions Leavis was asking himself in frustration during the composition of *D. H. Lawrence: Novelist*, I sympathised; but his book nonetheless left me feeling uneasy and with a fairly long list of 'yes but's'. As a preliminary to beginning my volume of the biography, I had done some work on what are known as Lawrence's 'psychology books', *Psychoanalysis and the Unconscious* and *Fantasia of the Unconscious*. My admiration for these texts did not prevent the shock of seeing them referred to in Leavis's book as 'serene and lucid', with all the poise of 'sober intelligence'. Those struck me as strange terms to use of works in which, among many other startling claims, Lawrence peremptorily insists that the sun is kept in existence by mysterious emanations from human beings. What assertions of this nature illustrate is a leaning towards a lunatic fringe of broadly theosophical thinking which Lawrence may have self-consciously indulged in order to loosen the grip on him of late nineteenth-century rationalism (and, contrary to common opinion, he is in general full of common sense), but which in my view means that it is seriously misleading to call the thought to be found in the two psychology books either serene or lucid, and describe the intelligence they manifest as sober. A truth they both point to is rather that Lawrence is uneven, and this is no less true in his fiction than it is in his discursive writing, so that, although nearly all the quotations in *D. H. Lawrence: Novelist* justify the superlatives used to describe them (and the skill with which they have been selected is obviously one of the book's strengths), it would not be too difficult to put together a fairly fat anthology of passages which gave a quite different impression.

As far as Lawrence is concerned, the later Leavis appears to have had a difficulty in acknowledging that someone could, on isolated occasions, be a crank, a bigot or even a windbag and still remain a genius. Arguing in *The Great Tradition* that Lawrence is the worthy successor of the three novelists whose work gives rise to the book's title, he adds: 'I am not contending that he isn't, as a novelist, open to a great deal of criticism'. Yet there is very little sign of this criticism in *D. H. Lawrence: Novelist* and hardly any of that judicious weighing of pros and cons which distinguishes Leavis's treatment of George Eliot, James and Conrad. This inclination in him to abandon a lifetime of discrimination and ignore the weaker aspects of a writer's work seems to me related to the way he increasingly felt that in Lawrence he had found someone who could articulate or embody his own sense of how society had developed after the First World War. But there is something more than this which I think attracted him. A splendid early essay that helped to establish his reputation as a critic is called 'The irony of Swift'. This is a subtle demonstration of how few positive values lie behind Swift's satirical writings. What we have in them, Leavis argues, is 'probably the most remarkable expression of negative feelings and attitudes that literature can offer – the spectacle of creative powers ... exhibited constantly in negation and rejection'. He insists that in his view this makes Swift a lesser writer than he might have been. The judgement may seem strange. Why should writers not indulge their negative feelings, and what compulsion should they be under to also have positive ones? The question revolves round what might be called faith. At one point in *Women in Love* Ursula declares she thinks it is immoral to be unhappy and there are signs in both Leavis and Lawrence that they held a similar view about giving in to hopelessness about life. Certainly Leavis castigates T. S. Eliot for apparently having done so in *The Four Quartets*. At the end of his essay on Swift he writes, 'We shall not find Swift remarkable for intelligence if we think of Blake', and Blake is the poet he often invokes in order to pass an unfavourable judgement on Eliot. 'What ... can one say to enforce one's judgement that the effect of [Blake's] poetry is very far from the inducing of an acceptance of human defeat?', he asks. 'One can testify that the poet himself is not frightened and, further, there is no malevolence, no anti-human animus, no reductive bent, in his realism: nothing could be more unlike the effect of Swift'. The reason for all this, Leavis goes on, is that, unlike Swift (or Eliot), 'Blake believes in human creativity'. All this will seem a long way from Lawrence until one recalls that, for Leavis, Blake was in many ways Lawrence's most obvious predecessor and that what he calls here a belief in human creativity often appears in his commentaries as an aspect of the belief in what Lawrence termed 'life'. As he emphasises in *D. H. Lawrence: Novelist*, the important thing for Lawrence's characters, as well as for the author himself, is that they should keep themselves open to the mysterious sources of this life and not cut themselves off, as in *Women in Love* both Gerald Crich and Gudrun Brangwen do. Only then can human beings save themselves from misanthropic despair. This creed is one which Leavis embraces wholeheartedly. But so wholeheartedly that it seems to me he is willing to let pass various weaknesses in Lawrence's writing. On a number of occasions (that is), he takes the word for the deed because the text carries a message, or is imbued with a spirit, of which he so much approves. When I think, therefore, of how he might have responded to my volume of the Lawrence biography, it is not so much that I imagine him disapproving of particular judgements but that I feel he would have deplored its tone, and its often implicit characterisation of its subject's faith as no more than obstinately willed optimism.

EIGHTEEN

... AND ELIOT

T hat for most of my life I have been a teacher of 'English' would have both amazed and puzzled my father. Lawrentians are fond, perhaps over-fond, of a story Lawrence tells in one of his late autobiographical writings. His first novel having just been published, he showed a copy to his father who asked him how much he had been paid for it. When Lawrence told him fifty pounds, the dumbfounded response was 'Fifty pounds! An' tha's niver done a hard day's work in thy life'. No writer ever worked harder than Lawrence, and often under the most extreme difficulties, but there is a sense in which his father, who was down the pit well into his sixties, was of course right. There is all the difference in the world between physical and mental labour while another important distinction centres around the question of constraint. Work you impose on yourself, or which can be done in what is largely your own rather than factory or office time, is never hard in Arthur Lawrence's sense. As far as constraints are concerned, having to sit through endless meetings you know are mostly pointless or administer a course, examination, graduate school or even a department can definitely make university teachers feel that there are better ways of spending their time. Marking piles of essay may be tedious and there are occasions when teaching itself can be difficult. Almost the last seminar I taught consisted of about fifteen friendly girls, mostly from the Home Counties, whom I was trying to interest in Falstaff. Feeling there might be a rocky road ahead, I painted an imaginary picture of intense audience expectation at the first performance of *Henry IV Part Two*, after the success of its predecessor. As a huge fat man trundled onto the stage followed by his tiny page, everyone in the theatre, I suggested, would be agog to hear Falstaff's opening lines so that 'Sirrah, you giant, what says the doctor to my water?' must have brought the house down. It could well have done but the effect of this line on my students was nil and no English comic at the Glasgow Empire died more comprehensively than I did in trying to persuade them that Falstaff was not, as they tended to think, just a dirty and intemperate old man. At moments like these teaching feels like hard work but one always knows it really isn't and that the life-style of a university teacher is remarkably privileged.

The question is the return one might be able to offer society for that privilege or, to put the matter more personally, what possible purpose did I ever serve? Leavis himself, I remember somewhere having read, was inclined to feel towards the end of his life that he had wasted his time so how much truer might that not be for some of his pupils? Especially those who, like me, were bound to be haunted with a sense of belatedness? After all, I arrived at Downing as Leavis's career there was nearing its end. The glory days, when he was a fierce young critic ruffling feathers and re-drawing the map of English poetry, or a little later when *Scrutiny* was in the avant-garde of critical thinking, were by 1959 well and truly over. After the Richmond lecture, he became much more of a social critic and the way he begins to repeat himself in the pieces collected together in *Nor Shall My Sword* is indicative of someone who feels mildly desperate and is conscious of having become marginalised. To be a Leavisite in the 1960s and '70s, when the 'theory' revolution was gathering speed, was certainly to be belated and that feeling was strengthened if you happened also to be, as so many of us were, from a grammar school. With the egoism of youth, I had always assumed that the grammar school I attended, with its Latin motto (*sto ut serviam*) and its division into 'houses' (without there being a boarder anywhere in sight), represented a permanent fixture of British society. Wasn't it after all the case that Shakespeare went to one? Yet in the form I knew it, my school really dated from the 1944 Education Act and it was to disappear in the late 1960s when the Labour government began subsuming most of the grammar schools into the comprehensive system. To be therefore one of their products, as well as a Leavisite, risked seeming doubly behind the times.

My education at Downing was meant to inculcate capacities which I could then help to stimulate in others. But what criteria were there to establish that I did in fact possess them, and how could their effect on and in others be demonstrated? Everything depended on a consensus of qualified third-parties, and it was easy to see that, in the adjective, the essential question was begged. Once my students had decided that Falstaff's opening lines in *Henry IV Part Two* were not impressive, there was no more to be said. On the assumption that the capacities I mention really did exist, I had increasingly the feeling that, in any case, they were becoming redundant. Along with *The Wheelwright's Shop*, one of Mrs Leavis's favourite, non-literary books was *Middletown*. Published in 1929, this was a study by a couple called the Lynds of the sociological and cultural effects of industrialisation on a small mid-Western American town. At one point, having described the remarkable artistry of the glass-blowers in a particular factory, they note how the introduction of new machinery after 1900 rendered a 'hand process that had come down largely unchanged from the early Egyptians as obsolete as the stone axe'. Literary criticism in a Leavisian mode could sometimes feel as if it were going the way of glass-blowing, or a thousand other skills the world no longer had any use for, the difference being that although the majority of those may have become useless, they were at least still clearly and objectively demonstrable.

In the 1970s, and later, there was an upsurge in the popularity of the 'campus novel', several of which included satirical portraits of recognisable Leavisites, adrift in an alien world. Perhaps the most memorable of these was not however in any novel but in Simon Gray's play, *Butley*. Gray was still in Cambridge when I arrived there, not at Downing but closely associated with the Downing group: he was a good friend of Ian McKillop, who would eventually write a biography of Leavis. *Butley* was his most successful play and deals with a day in the life of a young English lecturer of that name (Gray himself lectured in English at London University before becoming a full-time writer). In the course of the action, Butley suffers a series of hammer blows to his self esteem: the wife from whom he is separated tells him she has decided to move in with one of his friends; the young man who shares both his office and house, and for whom he seems to have had and may still have strong sexual feelings, turns out to be leaving both places; and a much older female colleague he has been used to patronising, tells him that she has finally finished her book on Byron while his own writing is clearly at a standstill. These and other misfortunes would attract the audience's sympathy were he not someone whose self-disgust easily turns outwards into scorn for others. The play is highly entertaining because Butley expresses himself with considerable wit and has an often dazzling line in scornful abuse; but he is in essence an unappealing character who spends much of the play fending off students who come to him to be taught, or drinking from a whisky bottle. The only course to take if you no longer believe in a job is to give it up but that is not always practical and *Butley* is a portrait of the kind of dysfunctional academic often still around in those years when it was written. They tended to constitute about ten per cent of any subject's teaching body. This was irritating but the 'accountability' measures designed to root them out were imposed uniformly and left the normally functioning ninety per cent with such a burden of mindless red tape that many decided that having to cover and compensate for wayward colleagues had been in the end less troublesome, and less damaging to their profession as a whole.

One important reason Butley appears to be not only dysfunctional but a dysfunctional Leavisite can be found in his admiration for T. S. Eliot. There is in his office a blown-up photograph of Eliot with, the stage directions indicate, 'a smear across it and one of its corners curled'. Although he affects a fondness for the nursery rhymes of Beatrice Potter, Eliot is clearly his major intellectual interest. We learn during the play that he has been encouraging a student in his criticism of his female colleague's seminars, suggesting he should transfer to him for tuition in Eliot's poetry. We also learn that his young baby daughter is called Marina and at one point he quotes lines from the poem by Eliot with that title. When, in the play's finale, the young man who is in flight from his female colleague's teaching arrives at his door, he asks him to begin the tutorial by reading from 'Little Gidding'. That he then sends even this student away, treating him just as he has the others throughout the play, is a sign of not only personal breakdown but also of how completely he has lost faith in his mission as a Leavisite teacher.

'Marina' was for Leavis a favourite among Eliot's works and there are at least two recordings, one from the Cheltenham Literary Festival but another made in private, where he can be heard reading it with great feeling. It is a poem which encapsulates, or at least hints at, many of its author's most striking characteristics. What clearly helped to make Leavis feel it was what he calls 'unique and lovely' was its opening:

> What seas what shores what grey rocks and what islands
> What water lapping the bow
> And scent of pine and woodthrush singing through the fog

This is indeed lovely but typical of Eliot in that, although it can be associated with holidays he took as a boy on the Massachusetts coast, the location is left imprecise. The two lines which immediately follow – 'What images return? / O my daughter' – contribute to the uncertainty Eliot always likes to create in that it is hard for the ingenuous reader not to want to identify this daughter. The title of the poem leads most critics to associate her with Shakespeare's *Pericles*. In the moment of that play when the eponymous hero is finally reunited with his daughter Marina, he says, 'But are you flesh and blood? / Have you a working pulse, and are no fairy / Motion?' It has been claimed that these words are faintly echoed at the point half-way through Eliot's poem where he writes,

What is this face, less clear and clearer
The pulse in the arm, less strong and stronger –
Given or lent?

but if that is so, the connection seems remarkably tenuous. The paradoxes ('less clear and clearer', 'less strong and stronger') are again typical of Eliot. The *Four Quartets* are full of them and in his commentary on those poems Leavis is inclined to be critical. The ones here, however, met with his approval. For him, poetry was always able to convey what can be expressed in no other form and is unparaphraseable. Certainly all the various and conflicting attempts to paraphrase these lines, as well as those parts of 'Marina' which involve (either directly or indirectly) the word 'daughter', would confirm this view.

Between the lyrical opening of this poem and the lines that begin 'What is this face?', there is a short section in which Eliot illustrates his remarkable gift for describing the sordid pointlessness of most human life. Many of the most memorable lines in the *Four Quartets* – the scene in the underground from the third section of 'Burnt Norton' would be a good example – are in this general mode. While not denying their impressiveness, Leavis is usually inclined to take them as evidence that Eliot is (to use the Lawrentian shorthand) 'anti-life' or that, unlike Blake, he denies 'human creativity' and, since he is a creator himself, is thus trapped in a disabling self-contradiction. Perhaps the section in 'Marina' escapes this kind of criticism because Eliot's descriptions of what amounts to death in life – sitting in the 'sty of contentment', for example, or suffering 'the ecstasy of animals' – are then immediately described as 'unsubstantial', 'reduced by a wind, / A breath of pine, and the woodsong fog'. They are defeated, that is, by natural forces even though there is a hint of the theological when Eliot goes on, 'By this grace dissolved in place'. The theological is what Leavis objects to in the *Four Quartets*. He complains of Eliot's pessimism not recognising, or may be only refusing to appreciate, that he is a little like the evangelical preachers of the late eighteenth century who reduced their congregations to wailing despair with a grim picture of their life on earth so that they would then be more receptive to the salvation that was on offer. In his view, Eliot's particular version of that salvation ('The dripping blood our only drink / The bloody flesh our only food') was too unattractive to consider seriously.

His quarrel with Eliot grew fiercer the older he became. A number of personal factors were involved. He used to describe to us, for example, how Eliot had been very enthusiastic about an early essay, 'Mass civilisation and minority culture'; had commissioned a piece on the state of contemporary literary criticism for *The Criterion* (the literary journal he edited from the early 1920s until 1939); but had then rejected it. The reason for the rejection, according to him, was that what he had written had been too controversial, and he characterised Eliot's editorship of *The Criterion* as a long series of cowardly concessions to Bloomsbury and fashionable opinion. It was he who had inspired Leavis's attack on Milton so that he clearly felt betrayed when, for what he believed were largely worldly reasons, Eliot delivered a lecture to the British Academy in which he more or less recanted. In an early number of *Scrutiny*, Leavis had written disparagingly of Stephen Spender's poetry but when *Revaluation* appeared Eliot gave it to Spender to review, with predictable results. Leavis seemed to him, Spender wrote in *The Criterion*, 'not so much an example of the poet turned critic because he cannot write poetry as of the critic turned lecturer and don because he cannot write criticism.' He accused him of a prose that was 'dull and cumbersome' and of having consistently borrowed all his critical opinions from Eliot.

On one occasion around 1941, Eliot happened to be in Cambridge and called in on Leavis. He would describe this visit to us often, always beginning with Queenie protesting that he ought not to have let 'that man' into the house. It may be that Eliot felt he did have something to expiate since he stayed a long time – Leavis was struck by the small mound of cigarette ash his visitor began to accumulate on the hearth. What he was apparently seeking was some kind of reconciliation and an understanding that, circulating as he had done in a London literary milieu, there were bound to have been occasions when he might have seemed at odds with someone of his host's uncompromising opinions. This at least was Leavis's view of the situation and he was proud to tell us that 'Tom' had eventually been obliged to go away disappointed. Guilt is an obvious feature of Eliot's poetry. One has only to think of those wonderful lines in 'Little Gidding' (much admired by Leavis) where the ghost offers an ironic account of the three gifts 'reserved for age', the third of which is,

> the rending pain of re-enactment
> Of all that you have done, and been; the shame
> Of motives late revealed, and the awareness
> Of things ill done and done to others' harm
> Which once you took for exercise of virtue.
> Then fools' approval stings, and honour stains.

Some of the guilt Eliot felt may have been associated with Leavis, who hints as much in a written account of the 1941 meeting where he claims that certain remarks made to him then later appeared in that section of 'Little Gidding' from which I have just quoted. But he goes on, 'I was (with good reason) a major focus of the guilt-feelings expressed in *The Family Reunion*, the most revealingly personal of [Eliot's] works'. This is quite baffling in so far as everyone knew that, if there was anything in Eliot's life which might have caused him major guilt, it was the way he had separated from his wife and then helped to have her committed to a lunatic asylum. In *The Family Reunion*, there is talk of the central character having pushed his difficult wife overboard during a cruise. His guilt feeling is quite clearly linked to this incident (whatever its actual details), and there is in my view not the slightest trace in the play of any relationship analogous to that between Eliot and Leavis.

Leavis's strange conviction that he was often at the forefront of Eliot's mind did not prevent him from recognising that the poet he had begun by admiring so much had often more important problems to worry himself about. Over the years he elaborated a diagnosis of these, part of which he would express to us by saying that Eliot found it impossible to contemplate sexual relations between men and women without the help of Dante's Beatrice. He was also fond of referring to the article on the contemporary English novel which Eliot had published in a French journal and in which he said that, when D. H. Lawrence's characters made love, they lost 'all the amenities, refinements and graces which many centuries have built up in order to make love-making tolerable'. These startling words were indicative for him of personal difficulties increasingly apparent in Eliot's poetry, however much he might attempt to hide them. The penultimate and not very long section of 'Marina' (the whole poem stretches to only a page and a half) begins,

> Bowsprit cracked with ice and paint cracked with heat.
> I made this, I have forgotten
> And remember.
> The rigging weak and the canvas rotten
> Between one June and another September.

Here are what seem like traces of an autobiographical 'I', but they are characteristically elusive: the reader would have a hard time relating them in any certain way to the author. This elusiveness was a quality that Leavis appeared to admire or at least accept in Eliot's earlier verse. It was part of its notorious 'difficulty', which was not quite the positive obscurity of Mallarmé and his followers but which he appears to have felt was an inevitable feature of all truly modern poetry, a linguistic equivalent of the complexities of modern living conditions. By the time of his commentary on the *Four Quartets* however, what had been admirably or perhaps only necessarily elusive, had begun to seem to him damagingly *evasive*.

Leavis was in no doubt that what lay behind these poems was 'a personal need', an 'imperative personal concern', of which Eliot himself was not fully conscious. That he set out to analyse the need or concern with that qualification in mind is concurrent with what had become a growing disillusionment with Eliot's critical writings. Along with the work of I. A. Richards, these had provided the spur to Leavis's early career. He had frequently in the past acknowledged his debt to them, but the more he scrutinised their often gnomic utterances, the more empty he seems to have felt many of them were. In the second part of 'Tradition and the Individual Talent', there is the claim that 'the progress of the artist is a continual self-sacrifice, a continual extinction of personality', and that 'the more perfect the artist, the more completely separate in him will be the man who suffers and the mind which creates'. This is Eliot's famous doctrine of impersonality which is quoted approvingly in *The Great Tradition* but with which, in his commentary on the *Four Quartets*, Leavis will no longer have any truck. The essay in which the doctrine is enunciated, and from which he had initially profited a great deal, he describes in one of his later writings as 'pretentious, confused and unilluminating' while, in his commentary on the poems, he says that although Eliot's 'talent for being equivocal' may have been a sign of poetic strength in a poem like 'Marina', it becomes in the *Four Quartets* more like the 'gift for double talk' he had often displayed as editor of *The Criterion*. This is because he has a capacity for 'self-deception and evasion' which denies him 'a completeness and clarity of insight into himself'. Leavis cannot have found it easy to make these adverse judgements: the difficulty he had in changing his mind is evident in his inability to be entirely open about how he had come to accept Dickens as one of his country's greatest novelists. The problem was that Eliot's distinction was inextricably entangled with Leavis's own sense of himself as a literary critic so that the progressive discovery of what appeared serious weaknesses meant a difficult re-ordering of his own value systems. That was why it was so important to have Lawrence on hand to help him with the task.

NINETEEN

EPILOGUE

In matters intellectual, I have been lucky enough to have known three exceptional individuals. Enright sits uneasily among them because he always made such efforts to appear ordinary; but his publications speak for themselves. It is a coincidence that the second person happened to be a colleague of Enright's in Singapore before coming to Kent. Frank Cioffi was a six-foot-four American who could never pass for ordinary and who had an astonishing grip on his audience whenever he lectured. He would shamble into the lecture hall, explain very clearly a philosophical issue that interested him and then keep everyone both intrigued and entertained (he could be very funny) with his explorations of it. The whole performance appeared to be extemporised, although it had always been carefully thought through beforehand. I can remember eagerly waiting for him to appear in one of the lecture theatres in Kent that would have been packed to the rafters, had it had any. There was a perceptible moan of disappointment when the philosophy professor of the day came in to announce that there had been an alteration in the programme which meant that he would be giving the lecture instead of Cioffi. He then made the mistake of saying that anyone who wanted to leave was free to do so. Although he was not a favourite among his colleagues, those of us who were also members of staff felt a professional duty to stay put; but the crowds of students had no such scruples and melted away like snow in warm sunshine.

Cioffi eventually moved from Kent to a chair in Essex but he returned to Canterbury after his retirement so that I was able to get to know him very well. He had achieved a modicum of public fame as a pioneer in what proved to be an effective dismantling of the theoretical framework of Freud's writings. His objections to the key concepts were not on the usual Popperian grounds. Recognising that there was a world of discussion where the criteria appropriate to scientific discourse were not appropriate, he showed that this too had its accepted rules and Freud could often be found breaking them. Cioffi's name became well known in Freudian circles but he used to give the impression that what he did there was a sideshow and that his real interest lay in the problems he was able to tease out of Wittgenstein's later writings. It was the number and variety of examples he could conjure up to illustrate these problems that made him so extraordinary for a non-philosopher like me. He had been brought up by his grandmother in a poor, Italian-speaking household in the Washington Square area of New York, had dropped out of high school before graduating and then joined the army as soon as he was old enough. After a period with the occupying forces in Japan, he spent some time digging up the corpses of American soldiers in France, so that they could either be sent home or properly buried. Stationed in Paris, he met there a young man who would later become well known to British radio listeners as Rabbi Lionel Blue. Because he himself was heading for Oxford, Blue suggested that Cioffi might use the GI bill to try to go there also. The essay he wrote as part of an entrance examination secured him a place at Ruskin College, but he was eventually able to move to St Catherine's. Many of the examples he later used in his speaking or writing were clearly related to his unusual cultural background before he arrived in Oxford. Sport figured largely along with radio programmes, films and popular culture of all kinds; but he was also extremely well read in English literature, interested in aesthetics (he wrote a commentary on the New Critics' 'intentionalist fallacy' still often referred to), and a great admirer of Leavis. While Cioffi was still at university, his involvement in societies which had invited Leavis to lecture meant that he met him once or twice, and although naturally and instinctively irreverent, he always spoke of him with great respect.

Leavis is of course the third individual on my list, and by far the most exceptional of them, although I never knew him in the way I did Enright and Cioffi. I can remember only a couple of private conversations, both of a most trivial kind; but I was nevertheless in contact with him on very many occasions. For Cioffi, Leavis was undoubtedly a genius. He made no bones about using that word, which I have always disliked because of its tendency to inhibit thought. It seems to me that the young Mozart was a genius because the powers he was able to demonstrate at such an early age are scarcely explicable whereas, in most cases, truly extra ordinary abilities are open to a rational investigation which is blocked by the use of the blanket term. Leavis himself, however, talked of genius freely enough although on one occasion when the word was publicly applied to him, he said that he judged it inappropriate. What made him certain of this, he went on, is that he had known two people 'at close range' to whom genius could be confidently attributed, one of them being Wittgenstein. Although he did not say so, the other he almost certainly had in mind was Eliot.

Leavis was obviously someone in whom great natural abilities of a conventional kind were united with a quite unusual sensitivity to poetic language. What made Cioffi call him a genius, however, was more the strength of his passionate commitment to the cause in which he believed, and his refusal to kow-tow to conventional feeling. This last attribute can sometimes be associated with various forms of egotism, as Molière is keen to show in his skilfully nuanced portrayal of Alceste in *Le Misanthrope*. Leavis's assumption that he was a central concern for Eliot in *The Family Reunion* might be counted as egotistical and, when I was in contact with him, the belief that he played a bigger role in the world than was in fact the case also manifested itself in the faint flickerings of a persecution mania. D. W. Harding recalled that in some of the letters Leavis sent him there was a 'thin paranoid streak … which most of the time, but not in extremity, he could keep well under the control of his high intelligence and alert social wariness'. There is a danger here in forgetting that, his early days especially, Leavis *was* persecuted, or at least constantly mocked, sneered at and excluded by a social and intellectual establishment he opposed. Although it could obviously be said that he brought much of this treatment on himself by his refusal to conform (who, when they are playing whist, Stendhal says somewhere, quarrels with the rules?), it took both courage and character not to be disheartened by fairly constant sniping and misrepresentation, and to continue to stand by what he believed. He was fond of telling us that Wittgenstein had once informed him that he had more character than intelligence. Affecting to have been outraged by this remark, he would describe in a semi-humorous manner how he had been tempted to knock the great philosopher down. Yet he did not fail to add that Wittgenstein had immediately gone on to say that 'intelligence can be picked up in the street' and, in his own fascinating 'Memories of Wittgenstein', he lays the stress on his subject's qualities of character and particularly his remarkable single-mindedness. There was in him, Leavis makes clear, an intensity of concentration that, for all his egotistical quirks, indicated an exceptional degree of impersonal and disinterested devotion to the intellectual aims he pursued. Something similar could be said of himself.

Given not only the hostility from most academics but also the general view of the state of British culture with which Leavis had started out in the 1920s, he needed all the character he could muster. One of the ways in which was later manifested that strong element of cultural pessimism enormously strengthened by the spectacle of the so-called civilised nations attempting to destroy each other in the First World War, can be suggested by a passage from an essay Eliot wrote in 1922 to commemorate the death of the English music hall star, Marie Lloyd. Noting that W. H. R. Rivers had attributed the depopulation of Melanesia to the fact that the 'Civilisation' forced upon the population had deprived it of all interest in life and that it was therefore 'dying from pure boredom', he went on:

> When every theatre has been replaced by 100 cinemas, when every musical instrument has been replaced by 100 gramophones, when every horse has been replaced by 100 cheap motor-cars, when electrical ingenuity has made it possible for every child to hear its bedtime stories from a loudspeaker, when applied science has done everything possible with the materials on this earth to make life as interesting as possible, it will not be surprising if the population of the entire civilised world rapidly follows the fate of the Melanesians.

There are many passages in *Fiction and the Reading Public* which echo these sentiments and there is no doubt that Leavis himself would also have subscribed to them. But then if things looked bad in the 1920s, how much worse must they have seemed in the 1950s and '60s? Without being able to see some cultural advantage in technological change, the picture could only appear grim and it must therefore have needed all Leavis's determination to retain that modicum of hope in the future, and in the powers of the human spirit, he so admired in Lawrence.

When Leavis referred to Eliot's essay on Marie Lloyd in our seminars, it tended to be ironically and with disdain. That may have been because he felt no American was qualified to talk authoritatively about British working-class culture. He could have felt that, since a frank and open sexuality was an important part of Marie Lloyd's act, Eliot was hardly the right person to be paying tribute to it. But the real reason he disapproved, it seemed to us (or to me at least), was that an intellectual of Eliot's standing had no business wasting his time on popular culture, and still less on trying to analyse what he was willing to call Marie Lloyd's 'genius' (I am sure he would have felt that the use of a word like that in relation to her was pretentious). In so far as this was indeed his objection, it gave me some personal difficulty. Thanks to my father's records, I had always been interested in the music hall and had even been to the Hippodrome in Salford to see one or two of its sad survivors plying their trade in shows with names such as 'Grin and bare it' or 'We have nothing on tonight'. More generally, I shared with most of my contemporaries some interest in the cinema and felt no particular objection to the different kinds of popular entertainment which, in the 1960s, were beginning to flood in from the United States. Although he had occasional American students (Marius Bewley being one), and many admirers in the States, there was in Leavis a perceptible anti-Americanism, as when he accused Eliot and Pound of having no proper historical sense of how English society had developed or, more obviously, declared Harry T. Moore disqualified by his nationality from discussing Lawrence with the necessary inwardness. But this was a superficial trait. At a more profound level, his attitude to America was identical to that of Lawrence who recognised it as the country where consumer capitalism was most advanced, and where one could therefore observe the probable end-results of what were still only tendencies in British society. For both of them, its influence was therefore uniformly bad and neither (I believe) could ever have conceived the possibility, which is all it is, that more might eventually be done for the creative future of the language known as English by, for example, the Ivy League graduates who write the script for *The Simpsons* than by the latest British novel or poem of any distinction.

We were of a generation already too deeply implicated in the Americanisation of our way of life to oppose it as resolutely as Leavis would have liked; but all that chiefly had to do with how we spent our spare time and did not therefore matter very much. A more pertinent example of what it sometimes meant to be an inadequate Leavisian involved reading books and came in the early 1960s with the appointment of Kingsley Amis to a fellowship in Cambridge. For Leavis, this was akin to Oxford having awarded P. G. Woodhouse an honorary doctorate (an event he referred to frequently): it showed how completely his own university had also lost sight of standards. I doubt he was familiar with much Amis – the only time I remember him mentioning a living British novelist was when he described how he had tried to persuade the master of Downing, a classical scholar, that Somerset Maugham was not a great writer. Perhaps if challenged on the subject he would have said what James did when, after having published an unenthusiastic review of *Sons and Lovers*, he was asked whether he had actually read the novel. I have, James apparently replied, 'trifled with the exordia'. Several of us had not merely trifled with the exordia of *Lucky Jim* but read it right through and found it very funny, a fact we failed to reveal as Leavis grumbled on about Amis's appointment. As the father of all campus novels, *Lucky Jim* would have many descendants, via Lodge and Bradbury in particular. They were funny also but left me more uneasy. To satirise aspects of a system you remain part of is fair enough; but to portray it as a complete farce, while still working within it and drawing your pay, seemed somehow wrong.

A few of us admired *Lucky Jim* and yet were perfectly clear that Amis was not Dickens. We remained certain, that is, not only that, in the words of the Oxford don who rebuked Robert Graves, we preferred some authors to others, but that some authors were also much better than others. Were that don alive today, he might be surprised to find how far events have conspired to justify him. His reasons for rebuking Graves were, I imagine, scholarly ones: the general field of English literature was laid out before students and their task was to study not evaluate it. Some such attitude has had to be maintained subsequently in order to help provide material for the research culture which was already fast growing in my time. The down-grading of criticism which the present dominance of that culture has necessarily brought (putting aside the question of value – what it is that is *worth* working on – makes an area of enquiry which might have begun to seem restricted illimitable) was assisted by a new spirit of relativism in both philosophy and politics. It became hard to say that Dickens was *better* than Amis, or Jane Austen better than the author of Downton Abbey, without positioning oneself as a member of that minority culture whose authority had in the past been so closely associated with social or economic privilege. At the beginning of Leavis's career this association was already beginning to break up but, in one of his very first publications, he nevertheless insisted that 'culture has always been in minority keeping' and went on: 'Upon this minority depends our power of profiting by the finest human experience of the past; they keep alive the subtlest and most perishable part of tradition'. This was elitism but one that grew from the apprehension of a future in which the only way to decide questions of value would be by counting heads.

Although it could no longer hope for the power provided by wealth or social standing, Leavis was conscious that to survive and exert any influence the minority he believed in had to have some kind of base. This was why he set such store by the university as 'a centre of consciousness and human responsibility for the civilised world'; and above all by an English school within the university. It must have been a blow to him when he reached an age which meant he had to retire from the Cambridge English Faculty, and it was one that would have been made more bitter when, after a quarrel over his successor at Downing, he felt obliged to resign his college fellowship. He would then have been without any institutional attachments had he not been invited to take up a visiting professorship at York (the new title did not break the strange habit which had grown up of referring to him as a doctor). While he was at York he continued to enjoy something of a vogue, receiving invitations to lecture in several other British universities but also from institutions in Ireland, Italy and the United States. He seems to have regarded these as opportunities to spread the word which it would be irresponsible to turn down.

It is hard to know what to say about the more social aspects of Leavis's teaching. For good or ill (and there must be something of both in Eliot's 'cheap motor-cars'), the powers he feared have triumphed so completely that there seems no more chance of resisting them than fish have of changing the water they swim in. The university as a centre of consciousness and human responsibility is easier for me to think about. For much of my time in higher education, there was between universities and the ordinary commercial activities of the nation a gap, artificially maintained perhaps but nonetheless perceptible. More recently, the interpenetration has become much closer so that now universities are evolving into vocational training centres which compete with each other for custom and are run on a system of profit and loss. More and more, their students are being transformed into customers who affect the shape of the curriculum by already knowing what they like. In this context it is hard to see a role for 'Cambridge English', squeezed on one side by the cultural studies both the Leavises did much to foster, and on the other by literary scholarship. However much literary critical discussion of canonical texts still goes on at the university, and that is probably a great deal, it is difficult to imagine it has much future. Perhaps this does not matter, any more than it matters that the judges of the Booker Prize should have recently called for submissions to be more 'readable', or invented a category called 'the literary novel'. I hope, however, it is not just conditioned reflexes which make me want to mutter occasionally 'English ought to be kept up'. When Keats wrote these words he appears to have been thinking of the extent to which Milton's style was influenced by his familiarity with Latin. The idea that the best writing needs to be in touch with the lively, idiomatic rhythms of ordinary speech, Shakespeare being the chief model, was a key concept for Leavis and underlies the argument in his early attack on 'Milton's verse'. That has a striking degree of personal commitment – he liked to remind us that a pocket Milton was the one book he had carried with him throughout the First World War – and contains analyses of the Mulciber passage in *Paradise Lost*, and of an extract from *Comus*, which ought to be regarded as (to use one of his own favourite terms) classical.

In my first years as a university teacher, I was never keen to advertise my intellectual provenance. I wanted to do things in my own way and was annoyed that, once people became aware that I had been to Downing, they tended to feel that they knew beforehand everything that I was going to say. It seemed unfair that, while they may have been influenced by their teachers, they were not known by those teachers' names, followed by an unpleasant suffix. We did not, as I have said, like to be called Leavisites. Yet if I hear the word now, I tend to think of those terms in the language (Tory and Whig, for example) which were originally abusive but later adopted as badges of honour. When the friend who had suggested that an appropriate title for my book on Wordsworth would be *The Visionary Dreariness* learnt what this present one was going to be called, he said that it reminded him of Spike Milligan's *Adolf Hitler: My Part in his Downfall*. That gave me pause for thought. Setting aside the unanswerable charge of egotism, it seemed to me that I had indeed played some very minor role in the decline and fall of Cambridge English. There were, that is, a number of occasions when I failed to support Leavisian principles as vigorously as I might have done, either because I was uncomfortable with some of their social ramifications or felt that, in the way the university world was developing, trying to hang to this or that pedagogic structure or method had become a hopeless task. Hopeless it may well have been but if there is a better general approach to teaching English than the one Leavis advocated, or an attitude that provides more insurance than his did against the dangers of functional autonomy (that tendency of institutions to churn on regardless, quite cut off from any initial social aim or utility), I have not yet found them.

ACKNOWLEDGEMENTS

M y thinking back about Leavis has been greatly helped by Ian MacKillop's biography which was published in 1995. In that same year, MacKillop edited with Richard Storer a collection entitled *F. R. Leavis: Essays and Documents* which is full of interest. The author of the very thorough book on *Scrutiny* mentioned in my preface is Francis Mulhern (1979), and two good general accounts of Leavis are by Michael Bell (1988) and Anne Samsom (1992). There is a robust and philosophically sophisticated defence of the Leavisian approach in *The English Prophets* (2001) by Ian Robinson, the former pupil referred to on page 10 above and the source of my quotation from the Council for University English in the second sentence of my preface. Robinson has also made available on the internet an absorbing account of his contacts with Leavis. In 1984 Denys Thompson edited a collection of *Recollections and Impressions* of the Leavises which I have found useful, as I have also G. Singh's *F. R. Leavis: A Literary Biography,* which appeared in 1995. Just after I had finished these memoirs, Christopher Hilliard published his *English as a Vocation: the* Scrutiny *Movement* a book which, in addition to well researched discussions of the influence of the Leavises on secondary education and cultural studies, contains valuable information about what I have called above the Leavisian diaspora.

Three former pupils of Leavis, Howard Mills, John Wiltshire and John Worthen, were kind enough to read a first draft of these memoirs and make useful comments, as were Bernard Sharratt, Christopher Thompson, Ann Newton, Chris Joyce and Edward Greenwood (the author of the British Council's pamphlet on Leavis in their 'Writers and their Works' series). Over many years I was fortunate enough to be able to discuss my Downing education with Frank Cioffi. In the last years of his life, Cioffi became particularly interested in our relation to our past. The following reflection, which I found among his papers, provides what seems to me a fitting last word (the final reference is to the Browning poem which begins, 'Ah, did you once see Shelley plain?'):

> Someday in my own time there will come a Pharaoh 'who knows not Joseph' and, though I did not know him very well myself, the prospect saddens me for I define myself at an intimate level by the lives I did not quite manage to lead, the circles I never penetrated, the aspirations which were unfulfilled and so will be left with no-one to understand what it was I feel I have missed, who it was that I might have seen plain and failed to.

INDEX

Aesop 4

Addison, Joseph 8

Attenborough, Richard 33

Aeschylus 64

Aquinas, Thomas 95, 112, 113

Amis, Kingsley 101, 141, 142

Arnold, Mathew 4, 26–7, 65, 82, 101

Austen, Jane 17, 37, 42, 48, 70, 107, 142

Bach, J. S. 24, 34

Balzac, Honoré de 5 (*La Peau de chagrin*),
    83, 91–2, 94

Barthes, Roland 93–5, 97

Baudelaire, Charles 113

Bayley, John 110

Beard, Derek 11, 71

Beckett, Samuel 120

Beljame, Alexandre 8

Bennett, Arnold 19

Berlioz, Hector 34

Berthoud, Jean-Marc 77–8, 81, 100, 112

Bewley, Marius 141

Blake, William 95, 127–8, 133

Bloch, Ernst 24

Blue, Rabbi Lionel 138

Borgnine, Ernest 3

Bottrall, Ronald 101

Bowra, Maurice 51–2, 53

Bradbrook, Muriel 33, 42, 86

Bradbury, Malcolm 141

Bradley, A. C. 109

Bridges, Robert 27

Browning, Robert 18, 25, 32

Burke, Edmund 79

Burns, Robert 35

Butler, Samuel 17

Byron, Lord George Gordon 9, 39, 91,
    131

Calderón, Felipe 113

Carey, John 17, 20

Cavell, Stanley 24

Cecil, Lord David 16, 72

Chabrol, Claude 63

Chadwick, Henry 28

Chaplin, Charlie 9, 56

Chapman, George 113

Chaucer, Geoffrey 59, 85

Cimarosa, Domenico 34
Cioffi, Frank 93, 137–8, 139
Cobbett, William 23–4
Compton, Dennis 11
Connolly, Cyril 48
Conrad, Joseph 20, 127
Constantine, Learie 31
Cowper, William 70
Croce, Benedetto 113

Dante, 112, 113, 135
Davie, Donald 101
Davies, Scrope Berdmore 39
Davies, W. H. 10
Derrida, Jacques 95, 96, 97
De Quincey, Thomas 10
Dickens, Charles 17, 19–20, 23, 40, 50,
    51, 57, 64, 88–9, 119, 136, 142
Works:
    Dombey and Son 20, 28, 88
    Hard Times 20, 88
    Little Dorrit 20, 51, 88
    Oliver Twist 91
Donizetti, Gaetano 34
Donne, John 112
Dostoevsky, Fyodor 64
Duns Scotus, John 95

Eagleton, Terry 52, 119
Edel, Leon 99
Eliot, George 16, 17, 20, 40, 50, 71–2,
    107
Eliot, T. S. 8, 10, 12, 20, 21, 35, 48, 49,
    50, 52, 57, 64, 70–1, 73, 80, 85, 101,
    120, 122, 127, 128, 132–6, 139, 140,
    141, 143
Works:
    After Strange Gods 48–50
    Burnt Norton 57, 133
    East Coker 85
    Family Reunion, The 135, 139, 140,

Four Quartets 73, 80, 127, 132, 133,
    136
Little Gidding 10, 132, 134
Marina 132–6
Tradition and the Individual Talent
    21, 136
Waste Land, The 8
Ellrodt, Robert 75–6
Enright, D. J. 100–2, 110, 124, 137, 138

Falstaff 46, 86, 129–30
Fielding, Henry 17–18
Flaubert, Gustave 62
Fluchère, Henri 78–9, 80
Foucault, Michel 95, 96, 97
Francis, Connie 40
Freud, Sigmund 92–4, 122, 138
Fry, Stephen 15, 30, 35

Gale, John 5
Gehardi, William 69
Giono, Jean 78
Goethe, Johann Wolfgang von 119
Goldberg, S. L. 103, 104, 111
Gordon, G. S. 85–6, 99
Graves, Robert 18, 44, 142
Gray, Simon 9, 131–2
Greer, Germaine 39
Grotowski, Jerzy 76

Haddon, A. C. 85
Harding, D. W. 34, 79–80, 139
Hare, David 119
Hardy, Thomas 25, 50
Harrison, Jane 8
Heidegger, Martin 96–7
Henry of Navarre 90
Holloway, John 1–2, 4–6
Holroyd, Michael 124
Homer 26
Hopkins, Gerard Manley 27

Hough, Graham 2, 3–4
Hunte, Conrad 31
Husserl, Edmund 96
Huxley, Aldous 124

Ibsen, Henrik 68

Jack, Ian 2, 82, 83
Jacobson, Howard 7, 13, 31, 70
James, Clive 17
James, Henry 20, 51, 62, 73, 88, 98, 99,
    118, 127, 141
James, Jimmy 46–7
Johnson, Samuel 21, 65, 72, 120
Jonson, Ben 51, 52, 92 (Jonsonian)
Joyce, James 2, 166 (*Ulysses*), 120

Keats, John 143
Kerr, Deborah 3
Keys, John 59
Kinkead-Weekes, Mark 86, 123, 124,
    125
Kipling, Rudyard 30
Klingopolus, G. D. 99
Knights, L. C. 79, 80, 108, 109, 111

La Fayette, Madame de 63
La Rochefoucauld, François de 62, 95
Lacan, Jacques 93, 94, 95 (Lacanian)
Lamb, George 39
Lancaster, Burt 3
Larkin, Phillip 94, 101, 120
Laughton, Charles 47, 48
Lawrence, D. H. 17, 36, 46, 48, 49, 50,
    51, 52, 63, 71, 73, 78, 84, 86, 102,
    101, 120, 123–8, 129, 135, 136, 140,
    141
Works:
    Apropos of *Lady Chatterley's Lover* 46
    England My England 3
    Etruscan Places 125

Fanny and Annie 48–50
Fantasia of the Unconscious 126
Lady Chatterley's Lover 16, 125, 126,
    128
Mornings in Mexico 125
Plumed Serpent, The 125
Princess, The 125
Psychoanalysis and the Unconscious
    126
Rainbow, The 8, 71, 78, 86, 120, 123,
    126
Saint Mawr 125
Sea and Sardinia 123
Sons and Lovers 141
Studies in Classic American Literature
    125
Virgin and the Gypsy, The 125
Women in Love 70, 120, 123, 125,
    126, 127, 128
Lawrence, Frieda 63
Lawrence, Saint 84
Leavis, F. R. *passim*
Works:
    Common Pursuit, The 11, 18, 28, 108
    Culture and Environment 15
    Great Tradition, The 11, 16, 17, 19, 23,
        37, 73, 88, 127, 136
    Irony of Swift, The 127
    Mass Civilisation and Minority Culture
        133
    New Bearings in English Poetry 11
    Nor Shall My Sword 130
    Revaluation 11 75, 95, 97, 124, 134
    Sketch for an English School 87
Leavis, Q (Queenie). D. 15, 37–8, 40–3,
    44, 45, 51, 57, 78, 81, 85–6, 99, 131,
    134
    Fiction and the Reading Public 15, 43,
        57, 140
Leavises, the 15, 41, 44, 51, 57, 81, 84,
    95, 100, 143

Lejeune, Philippe 94
Lewis, C. S. 26
Lloyd, Marie 140
Lincoln, Abraham 11
Lodge, David 141
Lubitsch, Ernst 47
Lucas, F. L. 44, 51, 57
Lucretius 112, 113
Ludowyck, E. F. C. 100
Lynd, Staunton and Helen Merrell 131
Lynn, Vera 53

Maillard, Michel 62–3
Mallarmé, Stéphane 64, 113, 135
Marsh, Derick 103–4, 111
Mason, H. A. 1, 4, 5, 24, 99
Maugham, Somerset 141
McKillop, Ian 131
Melbourne, Lady (Elizabeth Lamb) 39
Melia, Joe 33
Merimée, Prosper 107
Milligan, Spike 144
Milton, John 11, 20, 94, 143
Molière 63, 79, 139
Moore, Harry T. 141
Mozart, W. A. 34, 119, 138

Napoleon 77, 83 (Napoleonic)
Nashe, Thomas 23, 24, 42
Nehls, Edward 110
Newman, F. W. 27
Newton, John 1, 5, 13, 32, 35, 99, 108–9
Nietzsche, Friedrich 14
Nunn, Trevor 33

O'Brien, Connor Cruise 79
Oretaga y Gasset, José 69
Osborne, John 37

Painter, George 124
Parker, Ross 53

Pascal, Blaise 56, 117
Paton, Alan 104
Pope, Alexander 26, 35, 70, 72, 86, 119
Popper, Karl 57, 138 (Popperian)
Poulet, George 91–2
Pound, Ezra 2, 101, 141
Priestley, J. B. 17–18
Proust, Marcel 17, 24 (Proustian), 94, 124, 125

Quiller-Couch, Arthur 17

Racine, Jean 64 (Phèdre), 65, 94
Raglan, Lord 8
Raleigh, Sir Walter 99
Randall, Frank 46–7, 48, 50
Rawicz, Piotr 76
Richards, I. A. 22, 41, 136
Richardson, Samuel 17, 102, 122, 123
Richmond, Admiral Sir Herbert William 67
Rivers, W. H. R. 140
Rochester, Earl of 14
Rosenberg, Isaac 80
Rossini, Gioachino 34
Rousseau, Jean-Jacques 6
Rylands, G. H. W. ('Dadie') 51

Sainte-Beuve, Charles Augustin 4–5
Salingar, L. G. 82–3
Sand, George 83
Sarony, Leslie 47
Sartre, Jean-Paul 61, 91, 95
Saussure, Ferdinand de 93 (Saussurean)
Sewell, Brian 45
Shakespeare, William 20, 23, 33, 57, 65, 86, 118, 119, 130, 143
Works:
    Antony and Cleopatra 28, 108
    Othello 107–8

Macbeth 108
Measure for Measure 108
Hamlet 108
King Lear 108
As You Like It 111
Much Ado about Nothing 111
Henry IV Part Two 129–130
Pericles 132
Shapira, Morris 34–5, 111, 114
Shelley, Percy Bysshe 20, 95, 96
Simmel, Georg 96
Sinatra, Frank 3
Smith, James 111–12
Snow, C. P. 68–72, 88
Sobers, Gary 31
Southampton, third Earl of 59–60
Spender, Stephen 134
Starobinski, Jean 91–2
Steele, Richard 8
Stendhal 6, 76 (Stendhalian), 91, 92,
    107, 110, 122, 139
Stevenson, J. 45–6
Strachey, Lytton 124
Strauss-Kahn, Dominique 74
Sturt, George 55–6
Swift, Jonanthan 118 (*Tale of a Tub*),
    127–8
Swinburne, Algernon Charles 14

Taine, Hippolyte 98
Tanner, Michael 96
Tasso, Torquato 113
Tawney, R. H. 54, 56

Theobald, Lewis 86
Thompson, Denys 15, 21
Tolstoy, Leo 64
Traversi, D. A. 108, 109, 111
Trilling, Lionel 19
Trotsky, Leon 55

Valéry, Paul 64
Veaux, Erik 76–7
Verdi, Guiseppe 34
Virgil 113

Warner, Sylvia Townsend 110
Waugh, Evelyn 46
Wellek, René 95
Wellington, the Duke of 27
Whitehead, Alfred North 113
Wilde, Oscar 19
Wilkins, William 10
Williams, Raymond 81, 83
Wiltshire, John 37, 38, 40, 43, 86
Wittgenstein, Ludwig 26, 33, 96, 138,
    139
Woodhouse, P. G. 141
Woolf, Virginia 40–1, 44, 45, 49, 120
Wordsworth, William 63, 65, 70, 71
    (Wordsworthian), 94, 95, 113, 119,
    122, 123, 124, 143, 144
    Prelude, The 28, 94, 122
Worsley, T. C. 5, 30, 31
Worthen, John 123, 124

Yeats, W. B.